Winning With God

How To Win Life

Juma Salim

ISBN: 9798336590999

DEDICATION

I dedicate this book to the special people in my life who have challenged me to grow. In memory of my beautiful mother, who prayed for my salvation and taught me the importance of putting God first in all things. Your humbleness and ability to serve others were truly gifts from God. Every person you encountered, you gave the gift of love and the opportunity to know Christ. In times of discomfort, you enabled me to see the good in any situation. Honestly, your death caused me great grief; however, it has also given me the strength, courage, and sound mind to overcome my deepest fears.

To my beautiful daughter Imoni, thank you for always being you and always pursuing your dreams with relentless drive. To my oldest son Rai'Quan, words cannot express how much I love you and how much you mean to my life. Remember, no matter what you face in life, always pray, and seek God's will for your dreams. Lastly, to my youngest son Jacob, you have been God's second chance in my life. Every trial, tribulation, and setback has strengthened my character, resilience, and faith. Together we have grown and learned that life happens and how we react will determine the outcome.

Every family has one person that the elders deem worthy of carrying the baton to the next generation. Words cannot begin to describe how hardworking my sister Sonya is; you have listened to all my crazy ideas, goals, and dreams. When giving up crossed my mind, you have always cheered me back into the fight. When other people gave up and turned their backs on me, you stood in the gap on my behalf and never stopped believing in me. Thank you!

We all have someone in our lives who displays superhero characteristics; they motivate us and display acts of heroism. To my brother J.D., thank you for your ability to live in your truth and dare to be different. Overcoming fear and living on the edge has always been something I admired about you. Thank you for teaching me how to live a courageous life. You are loved, cared for, and much needed.

Every great fighter has a hype man; this person is skilled and proficient in helping the fighter endure to the end. My corner man is the greatest friend and brother in Christ a man could ask for. Reggie Redmon is a pastor, father, husband, and brother. Your spiritual mentorship and short sermons have lifted me from some of the darkest times in my life, and I am forever grateful.

There are so many people I would like to thank who have inspired me on this journey; it is difficult to capture those names in this limited capacity. You have not been forgotten, and I look forward to seeing all your wonderful faces again. Life without a solid foundation is an unstable life; finding your tribe enhances your lifestyle. During challenging times, your tribe will help you along your journey with the resources you need to be successful. Never forget your tribe; a heart of gratitude is a healthy heart.

Table of Contents

INTRODUCTION

Everybody wants to win; it doesn't matter what level of life you may be on, winning is the name of the game. Nobody has a problem with winning; people are not going around complaining about the deal that propelled their career. At an early age, we are conditioned by our parents to perform and produce. From the time we are conceived to our actual birth, our parents created a blueprint for our success. While most kids struggled to sit up, crawl, or even take their first steps, my struggle was balancing this giant head on my tiny shoulders. (LOL)

Too often in life, we look for the familiar things that help us trust in our ability and not the will of God. When life gets tough, and trials and tribulations enter your life like a massive storm, where do you put your trust? How do you find balance when the winds of life are tearing your house apart? One of the first lessons of life that we all can relate to is how to balance ourselves. No matter how many times we have fallen, our parents, friends, and family have encouraged us to get back up. Sometimes staying down doesn't mean you have given up; it just means you need more time to regain your balance.

As kids, our ability to learn how to balance our bodies would become a direct connection of our next phase in life. Learning how to balance life is a daily process that requires honesty, self-care, and relentless focus. To be honest, the pressure to perform is often the stumbling block that hinders us from reaching the next level of our lives.

The goal in life is to be better than you were the day before and to press forward toward the finish line in hopes of being rewarded. What are your current goals in life? What stage of life are you currently in? When life becomes overwhelming (and it will), how do you deal with the pressure of staying balanced?

Learning how to gather your footing in life becomes a process that repeats itself. We aim to perform and excel in whatever it is we do. The parents we once performed for are now our family, friends, co-workers, supervisors, neighbors, kids, and social media connections. As we move forward throughout the book, we will look at various aspects of how balancing our bodies works. Does your current state of mind line up with your body? What does the communication signal look like between your mind, body, soul, and spirit? What type of dialogue or messaging are you sending and saying to your inner being?

Our mind and body react differently according to our thoughts, behavior, and actions, which directly affect our physical body. This book is about how to perform on all levels, how to succeed from the inside out, and how to put God first in all that you do. Winning is what this race is all about, and knowing when, how, why, and what we are winning for is far more important. If you are playing this game called Life to please yourself or others, you are bound to lose every time. Things change, people change, seasons change, but God remains the same.

God is the same year-round, day in and day out; God is eager to see you perform your best. The real winning in life starts when you understand that apart from God, your wins are merely individual merits. The game of life is about sharing your gifts, talents, insight, and experiences with the people around you. There is nothing better in life than winning in the right places.

Every loss should teach you something new, and learning new things challenges you to grow. With every bad shot you take in basketball, you gain more confidence by committing to your shot. From the form to the release, the rotation of the ball, and even your follow-up position after the shot increases your success. The more that you practice you begin to form a habit, and with every shot, you start to understand that you will make good shots.

The more you train, the more your skills start to develop, and you start to understand the what, when, where, and how of the game of life. Winning with God is not easy; you need more than a big heart and a few prayers. This fight is spiritual and not physical, and if it were easy, others would get on board. You will have to be intentional about everything you do, even in the small tasks that may seem meaningless. Those small insignificant moments are the ones that God watches the closest. As we journey through different experiences throughout the book, the final question will entirely be up to you. Are you winning with God?

CHAPTER 1

The Balancing Act

We are living in a world where it seems that everything is communicating a message to us. Radio ads, television commercials, direct mail, text messages, and emails play a key role in our daily lives. Social media ranks high on the list of things that communicate a message; every day, a new app or media outlet streams the newest information right into the palm of our hands. What if I told you that the more noise we take on, the less we can hear from God?

There are countless people across the United States who work two jobs, attend school, and make time for their kids'. Let's just say having no energy in these cases is an understatement. There are only twenty-four hours in a day; let's break that number down into a daily routine. All right, let's say you worked twelve hours, which means you have only twelve hours left to do the other things you need to do. Grocery shopping is next on our list. If you're like me, you want to save money. So, it could take up to two hours to find the best deals in the store. Oh, the joy of grocery shopping; now you only have ten hours left. Next, you hit the gym; a solid hour of intense working out only leaves you with nine hours.

Today just happens to be a self-care day, and depending on the barber or stylist, it could be an hour wait and another hour to get done. You have only eight hours left.

You rush home to cook, but first, you must navigate through an hour of traffic. Now, you have less than seven hours. Your meal takes an hour. Next, you do homework with the kids. You catch up with your spouse and clean the kitchen. Then, you tidy the house, and the list goes on and on. Suddenly, the game clock sounds, and the day is over. Where did the time go?

Our daily activities have increased while the time that we must complete our tasks has decreased. There is more to do each day as we find ourselves buried with task after task to further our careers, goals, dreams, and to take care of our families. It can be overwhelming, which increases stress, health issues, lack of rest, and mismanagement of the time and resources that we have been given. What happened to spending quality time with our families, and long walks in the parks.

Communicating our thoughts, feelings, and emotions to one another has turned into memes, short texts, social media, and technology. Life has become a rat race, which often leaves us broken, as we tend to neglect what we should value most. Finding balance in a world that has become obsessed with selfies, success, and going viral has driven us apart from reality, each other, and God.

With so much going on, it is easy to forget that this life is temporary, and tomorrow is not promised. We must get back to valuing the time we have with one another and becoming more aware of the people around us. Just the other day, I was downtown and noticed everybody walking around with their heads down like zombies glued to their mobile devices. Millions of people feel alone and long to share their stories. They need to know someone cares; your short interaction with them could change their lives. Finding the balance we need starts with God.

For the last two years of my life, I have realized that the more God I added, the less worried, stressed, and overwhelmed I felt. Life is a blessing, not a problem or situation that must be figured out; we must learn to say no to the voice of busyness and say yes to the voice of God. Life is a blessing, not a project. In God, there is perfect peace; His will has everything you need, want, and desire. First you must learn to surrender your will and allow Him to lead.

According to the Merriam-Webster dictionary, the word balance has several meanings. However, we will examine just a few that are related to our subject matter. *"It is a means of judging or deciding, a counterbalance weight, force, or influence, stability produced by an even distribution of weight on each side of a vertical axis."* It also can be defined as *"a form of mental and emotional steadiness, dealing with the mind."* Wow, right there is where you should be shouting because who can balance your life better than God?

Everything that defines the word balance is who God is and has always been in every situation in your life. It seems like yesterday that you were about to lose your mind. You prayed to God. He not only provided a way out but also a sense of peace. That, my friend, is balance. It is important that before we move any farther, we line up the definition and the meaning of the word balance with the word of God: *"Trust in the Lord with all your heart, and do not lean on your understanding. In all your ways acknowledge Him, and He will make all your paths straight."* (Proverbs 3:5 NIV)

It is here we see that leaning on your understanding can and will produce imbalance. If you are leaning, then that means you are unstable in the distribution of your judging and deciding. Every time I thought I knew better than God, it weighed on me.

It caused me great stress, and I was an emotional wreck. In that condition, I had no power; there was no direct connection to the source, and just like the light you may be using to read this book, without a proper connection, let's just say there can be no progress.

Chapter 2

Fix Your Face

In the Bible, there is a story about a wealthy man named Job who, in my opinion, had every right to have an angry face and an outward look on life. Job had everything a man could want: family, land, livestock, servants, and he was an upright man in God's eyes. In Job chapter 1, we see that he was a man with great character and went before God on behalf of his kids in case they had sinned in their hearts against God. How many times have you gone to God on someone else's behalf?

We will discuss that in a later chapter; right now, let us continue to look at how the story of Job unfolds. Satan was permitted to test Job, believing that Job would curse God to his face. Understand that "cuss" and "curse" are two different things; *"a curse is "the expression of a wish that misfortune, evil, doom, etc., befall a person, group, etc."* While "cuss" in American terminology is simply to *"say bad words or swear"* (di**ctionary.com**). Cursing God would be the highest iniquity (a form of sin) one could do.

God had put a hedge of protection around Job and all that he owned, and Satan wanted God to remove his hand from Job's life. It is important that we don't overlook the fact that when Satan approaches the heavenly council and God asks him where he had been, Satan answers the Lord, *"From roaming throughout the earth, going back and forth on it."*

This statement from Satan's mouth is powerful because it lines up with a later scripture in the New Testament. When we look at 1 Peter 5, there is a letter that was written that clearly warns the people of God just what the enemy does. In 1 Peter 5:8, the warning is clear: *"Be alert and of sober mind. Your enemy the devil prowls around like a roaring lion looking for someone to devour."* As we see, it's not good people that the enemy is after; he is after whomever he can devour.

Job was at the top of the hit list because God was pleased with his life, and His favor was on Job's life. As the story continues to unfold, four different servants come to Job to bear shocking news. First, he lost his oxen and donkeys, then another servant came and said he had lost his sheep when fire fell from the sky. Meanwhile, another servant comes to bear worse news, saying that his camels had been stolen. The final blow came when, yet another servant brought sad news saying a mighty wind had knocked down the house all his children were in, and no one survived.

At that moment, Job got up, tore his clothes, shaved his head, and went into worship saying to God, *"Naked I came from my mother's womb, and naked I will depart. The Lord gave and the Lord has taken away; may the name of the Lord be praised."* (Job 1:21 NIV) After all that happened to Job, he still did not blame God. Revisiting this story, I wondered about Job's heart. After losing everything, he still had praise for God. While preparing this chapter and revisiting the story about Job, it made me take a good look back over my life and ask myself how many major disasters happened in my life and what was the condition of my heart and mind? It's amazing that a story so sad can give us hope that no matter what happens in life, God still knows what is best and He deserves all the praise and glory.

Put yourself in Job's shoes; how would you have reacted? See, the difference between Job and most of us is that Job was more focused on the creator than the stuff that the creator had blessed him with. As I took a second to reflect and be transparent with my own life, I was broken beyond repair when my mother, grandmother, and grandfather all passed within a nine-month period. At first, I didn't want to believe it as I trembled holding the phone each time. I was hurt more than angry at first. As the reality of no more texts, phone calls, and visits became clearer, I was truly angry with God, and I said some crazy things in those moments.

All of these people played a significant role in my life and my mother was the woman who raised me, the woman who taught me about life, the woman who introduced me to God, and was my spiritual connection to God when my pride would not allow me to go to God myself. Life was unbearable and God had allowed all these things to take place as some sort of payback for all the wrong I had done. As time went on, I realized that in their absence, I became stronger and less dependent on those that I loved and more on a God who loved me more than I knew.

What in your life has caused you to turn your smile into an unpleasant disposition towards God? With all that goes on in our lives, we must learn to commit our hearts and minds toward God with the right attitude. We have to understand that God is in full control and His purpose is better than our plan. Our hearts and minds must be aligned continuously to His will and not our own. As we look back on the story of Job, his heart and mind were set on God.

If Job lived today, can you imagine how he would have felt as text message after text message rolled in like a hurricane ripping his very foundation away? He had lost everything he had worked for in what seemed like minutes. His story is even relatable today as you or someone you may know has lost it all or currently going through a storm that threatens to rip all they own away.

It was a beautiful Sunday morning in May of 2013 and though I had talked to my mom the night before, she said she was fine. My heart felt heavy because it seemed as if she was waging this fight alone. As my mother lay in a hospital bed in North Carolina, I was 800 miles away in Tennessee feeling helpless. At the time, I was working for a moving company and our payday was not until the next week. With no money, no real friends, or even close relatives, I could not see a way to get there to be by her side. That morning was different; I woke up heavy as if something were on top of me and it seemed as if the weight was unbearable. This feeling was so heavy I had to roll out of bed and fall to the floor to get up.

At the time, I had just moved back to Tennessee from Michigan, and I was staying with a friend's mother till I was able to get on my feet. My heart felt heavy, and it seemed as if something was wrong; as I opened the door to my room, I had to hold onto the wall just to make it up the hallway. Cynthia, my friend's mom, asked me if I was alright, and I remember telling her my experience with the heaviness I felt in my room. She immediately urged me to call home to see how things were going.

As I dialed the number, my heart was eager to hear my mother's voice. I wanted her to encourage me, even as she lay there not knowing what would happen next. The phone rang two or three times, and an unfamiliar voice answered, asking who I was. At this point, it had not dawned on me that anything was wrong. As I told the woman on the other end of the phone my name, she spoke to someone in the background and passed the phone. My sister took the phone with a soft and broken voice and said, "Juma, mommy is gone."

With all the strength I had left in me, I fought the thought of my mother being gone and kept repeating stop playing repeatedly until finally, I let go and the weight of death fell on me.

What seemed like minutes went by, and I found myself on the floor broken, sobbing, and angry. Life as I knew it had ended; nothing made sense, why now? My heart was broken, the pain zipped through my body, and nothing could soothe this crack in my heart. The 800-mile trip home was the longest drive of my life; the more I drove, the more tears poured out. At one point, I had to pull over because I could not stop the tears. Somewhere in the mountains between Tennessee and North Carolina, an eagle flew by the windshield so close that our eyes connected as it flew toward the right side of the car.

At that very moment, a cloak of peace came over me and it was at that very instance that my inner strength grew, and I was able to push through. An eight-hour trip turned into a 6-hour trip as I hit speeds of 110 or more, stopping for gas two or three times. By the time I arrived, it was night and as I walked into my sister's house, no words can describe the moment we had as we stood in her living room hugging and crying.

When it was time to say my final words, I confidently walked towards the casket, I stood there talking to her with every part of me fully attentive to this moment. As I finished my words, I leaned down and kissed her on the forehead knowing that this was one step closer to our final goodbye. Her body was cold and stiff, she looked at peace. That day I walked away knowing that God had a plan, and her transition was to empower me to do remarkable things.

After the funeral, I stayed at my sister's house for an extended time to put things into perspective and get back to the fight of my life. Life was different now and my mother was gone, and it was time for me to be a man, it was time for me to fix my face. Our strength comes from the memories we have made along the way, good or bad, and each battle we conquer gives us confidence that God is placing the right obstacles and fights in front of us to fulfill His purpose in our lives. The problem is our vision may not line up with God's perspective; we have limited vision and are often unable to see the dangers ahead.

Job's heart was set on pleasing God with or without materialistic possessions. We live in a world where the latest iPhone, Galaxy, Nike, or Jordan has become the central focus. We must get back to seeking God with the right face, surrendering our entire mind, being, and soul to seeking His will. Long before Job had the wealth of this world, he had learned to trust God on the road to his success. Learning how to trust God when you have nothing is called stewardship; a good steward knows how to be content with a little or a lot. Understanding that God was the source, Job was able to find a place in his heart to worship the Creator even during his pain and loss.

We must get our focus back on God for who He is and not what He can do for us. Have we forgotten that the things of this world are just temporary and that our eternal treasures are in heaven? God desires to see us living a life that is pleasing to Him no matter what condition we may find ourselves in.

Over the years I have met people who had nothing and people who had everything. What I have come to learn is that the people who have nothing will give you everything and the people who have everything will give you nothing.

Tomorrow is not promised so why are we so fixed on pleasing ourselves more than pleasing God? In Jeremiah 29:11(NIV) the scripture reads, *"For I know the plans I have for you, plans for welfare and not for evil, to give you a future and a hope."* As we look at this scripture the words *welfare* and *hope* are defined by Webster's Dictionary: welfare is related to *"the health, happiness, and fortune of a person or group."* While hope is related to *"a feeling of expectation and desire for a certain thing to happen."*

So, as we revisit the scripture using that definition of welfare and hope it reads, *"For I know the plans I have for you, plans for your health, happiness, and fortune, not for evil, to give you a future and a feeling of expectation and desire for a certain thing to happen."*

It takes the right attitude to receive the promises of God and all He has in store for us. Faith and hope go hand in hand and the words that proceed out of the mouth of God will not return void. We must learn to fix our face even when the storms of life bring destruction, even when we don't understand what is happening in our lives, we must remember the promise in Jeremiah 29:11.

If we trust God to do exactly what He said He would do, then we must learn to put a face of praise and worship on. Our face and faith should be a mirror image of each other, and our expectations should be set on the promises of God.

Chapter 3

Learning How to Lose

Nobody wants to lose because society has created an illusion that greatness is not associated with losing. The problem associated with this type of thinking is that nobody who has become great wanted to lose. Nothing happens overnight, and nothing happens without a reason.

Winning and losing are about timing. Floyd Mayweather fought the last fight of his career on August 26, 2017. It wasn't the hype or the money that made this one of the biggest fights of all time; it was the timing. Mayweather was forty-nine and zero; Conor McGregor was the UFC champion and crossed over for the fight of a lifetime. Both fighters had a legacy on the line from their respective platforms; however, win, lose, or draw, both fighters walked away with more than money could ever buy; it was about the experience.

McGregor is the only UFC fighter to date who has stepped outside the octagon and into the boxing ring to fight an undefeated world-class boxer. Unfortunately for McGregor, he lost; however, he learned a valuable lesson about his UFC style of fighting and boxing.

Every fight is different, and no matter how much you prepare, you will never know the outcome. McGregor lost because he did not have enough endurance to go the distance. Can you imagine being in the fight of your life and losing because you lacked endurance? You trained, ate right, sparred three or four times a day, lifted weights, and went on a massive cardio workout only to lose the fight.

The fight itself requires you to use every part of your being to finish strong. It requires your mind, hands, feet, body, heart, breathing, eyes, and movements. If every part doesn't work in unity, then your performance will not match the intensity of the fight, and you are bound to lose. If you think it requires a lot to win, just imagine how much it will take to defend.

Every level-up is a new battle, and each fight will be different. Each fight will require a different approach, a different frame of mind, and a different strategy. There are some things in life that you are not prepared for no matter how much you train, study, rest, eat, or run. Sometimes life just happens, and the best defense for those times often requires us to lose.

Perhaps, it's our pride or how others may view us after a loss that makes us want to avoid facing failure. Instead, we should learn from it, fix our mistakes, and seek a rematch. Just imagine how much further we would be in life if some of the battles we walked away from we stood up to. Maybe the rematch wasn't worth it; maybe we were satisfied with a draw. What if the fight was not even important enough to entertain? We all have a fight, and every fight is different. The problem is we often waste energy fighting battles that were never ours, which often leaves us drained.

McGregor fought a fight that was not his fight. He was in an unfamiliar ring, the time of the rounds were different, and he was restricted to only using his hands. Boxing gloves and UFC-style gloves are completely different. Boxing gloves enclose your whole hand, while UFC gloves just cover the back of the hand and the knuckles; the fingers are exposed.

This makes a huge difference because the weight of the boxing glove is heavier than the UFC glove, which adds weight to your hands and arms. Not only was the fight different, McGregor did not have access to the components that made him a successful fighter in the UFC. His style of fighting was catered to using his whole body, which caused him to be limited in this new fight. Not being able to use his whole body made a major impact on the type of fight he fought.

What types of fights are you fighting? Understand that there will be moments in life that will seem as though you have been limited. You will feel as though winning in a situation is not possible. We have been trained from the time of birth that winning is all you need to do to become successful. Winning is awesome, however, learning how to lose sharpens our core and builds up our focus.

On my journey, I have come to realize that the fight I face is not solely about me; it is about God's will for my life. The battles that I lost were to strengthen me and help me to become a stronger light. A loss is something that can be obtained again; it is a temporary area of setback that you must work on to strengthen. Defeat, on the other hand, is when you were not intentional in your actions by putting forth an effort. It was a deadline that you did not take seriously or an area in which you had the skill to do remarkable things and lacked confidence, so you ran from the challenge.

What area in life have you been avoiding or not been intentional about? We all have suffered from a loss that felt like defeat;

sometimes it is the loss that gives us the power to try again. Don't let defeat cause your setback; defeat is what has been the knockout blow that has taken a lot of dreams, visions, and good people out of the fight. It is defeat that often leaves you feeling powerless.

Learning to become transparent helps us to be honest, truthful, and aware of what we need to let go of. We serve a mighty God, and we must see ourselves as God sees us: whole, complete, full, confident, and victorious even when we face setbacks or stumble.

In Proverbs 3:5, it states, *"Trust in the Lord with all your heart and lean not on your understanding."* It may seem that things happen for no reason, but you must understand that God's plan supersedes our plans, and our time is not his time. In verse 6, it states, *"In all your ways acknowledge him, and he will make your path straight."* As you look at that scripture, remember that by being aligned with the will of God, you should know that with him all things are possible. He has total control over every situation in your life. He knows what you need, and if you have God, you have all the balance you will ever need.

Chapter 4

Face Your Fears

In the last chapter, we discussed learning how to lose. Let me point out that no one commits to or aims at a goal and then decides that they want to lose. Knowing how to recover after a loss makes the loss more about the experience than the actual setback. No one sets out to lose; we all have the intent on winning in our hearts and minds from the start. Our intentions are usually from a good place, and the desire to win is often genuine. But what if I told you that our fears often cause us to lose before we even get a good running start?

Faith and fear cannot occupy the same space at the same time; you either have one or the other. Remember that wherever fear is, love is not present, which indicates that there is no commitment. Too often we start with bold and strong faith; our confidence dwells in the idea of accomplishing our goal. However, as we get further into the fight, we start second-guessing our journey after just a few setbacks. You do know that our fears are based on thoughts, ideas, or events that have not even taken place. Do you know how that sounds?

What happened in our lives over time that caused us, as adults, to become so afraid? Remember, as kids, we were so fearless: climbing, jumping, running, and falling without a care in the world. We would fall and often bounce back up and keep playing.

Sometimes if our parents were present, we would cry, not because we were seriously injured but because we wanted them to know that we were embarrassed.

Somehow, as time went on and we grew into ourselves, we became so fearful of failing in life that we stopped trying. In the Bible, there are 60–70 verses that speak about faith and over 135 verses that speak about fear or being afraid. Only 22 verses mention the word fear, which is shocking because we often overlook these scriptures to hear stories about faith, confidence, and victory.

In order to win our battles, we must first face our fears. David was just a boy when he confronted Goliath, and he had no fear because he believed that God would deliver on the very words He promised. The scriptures use the word afraid, which is interesting because what I found in my research is that fear and being afraid operate together; you cannot have one without the other.

Being afraid is what triggers fear; fear has no power if you are not afraid. Let us go back to English class for a moment; a noun represents a person, place, thing, event, substance, or quality. While an adjective simply describes a noun, for example, big fear, little fear, fat fear, tall fear, weak fear, or strong fear. Isn't that ironic, that we would give fear power simply by what we add to it?

What have you given your power to? Is it fear of an old debt, an old friendship, a job that you are afraid of losing, or a relationship that is toxic and you feel afraid that you won't be able to function without it? If you have answered yes to any of these questions, then my friend, you realize you are living in fear. We must learn to fight with faith and not let fear have the upper hand, God has already given us the victory.

By boldly believing and confidently confessing that His Word is the foundation of our lives, we should be living out His Word. We should move with an attitude of expectancy no matter what we may face. The things that we are the most fearful of often hold the keys to our future. In 2 Timothy, chapter 1, verse 7, we have been given an advantage in the fight. It states, *"For the spirit God gave us does not make us timid, but gives us power, love, and self-discipline."* As we look at this scripture, we must first realize that we have been awarded a spirit from God. The very spirit that God has given us does not know fear or how to be afraid. If we experience fear, then we are not operating in the right spirit. We must go back to the drawing board and find out what has caused us to become afraid. Getting to the root of the issue is the first step we must take in facing our fears.

Maybe, it's something that you have not let go of in your life: the loss of a job, a failed marriage, a bad breakup, or even a failed business attempt. The only way to find the root of the problem is to be truthful and face the issue head-on. Life is an experience, and there is nothing we have done in life that can separate us from the love of God. By giving God all our mistakes, bad decisions, worries, and concerns, we become less burdened in our daily lives and more focused on the path set before us.

When we give God total access and control over our lives, we can live a life full of purpose rather than a life full of fear. Learning to control our feelings, thoughts, and actions helps end self-doubt by seeing ourselves as God sees us: strong, complete, and victorious. When we make a conscious decision to live a self-disciplined life, we become strong in the areas that the enemy attempts to attack. It all starts in our minds. If the enemy can infiltrate your thoughts with second-guessing, overthinking, and the what-if factor. No decision is what often leads us to failure. Don't become a prisoner in a world where you are totally free. Use your power and self-discipline to fight off the mental and spiritual attacks that the enemy attempts to use against your mind.

The enemy knows exactly how powerful you are, and if he can persuade you into thinking that you are not good enough, then he has won half the battle. It is the enemy's job to attack you; he knows how much power you have been given, and that is why he roams to and fro looking to pounce on every mind that is not strong. Your mind is a powerful weapon, and the enemy knows that if he can infiltrate your mind with negative thinking, then he can stop the amazing life God has ordained for you. It is important that you understand God's love for you, and you love yourself and others with that same love.

What are your thoughts about yourself at this very moment? Are they positive thoughts or negative thoughts? How you see yourself is vital to your growth. If you see yourself as weak or not good enough, then how do you think the enemy sees you? It all starts in your thinking. In Mark 12:30, we have been commanded to *"Love the Lord your God with all your heart and with all your soul and with all your mind."* The enemy will have a tough fight if we are obedient to the word that has been put before us.

In Romans chapter 12, verse 2, it speaks about renewing our minds and warns us not to conform to the world's patterns. It clearly states, *"Do not conform to the pattern of this world, but be transformed by the renewing of your mind, then you will be able to test and approve what God's will is, His good, pleasing, and perfect will."*

With technology and social media playing a significant role in our lives, we often see what others are doing and forget that God's plans for your life will look nothing like what the world offers. The pattern that the world has been modeled after has not been approved by God, which is why we must be transformed by our thinking.

Society has created a false sense of happiness through devices, jewelry, cars, and clothes. People chase temporary satisfaction with material possessions and lavish lifestyles. God's will for our lives can be described in Hebrews chapter 13, verse 5, which suggests by keeping our lives free from the love of money and being content in what we have that we can stand on the promise that God will never leave us or forsake us.

What is your greatest fear? Maybe you're fearful that you will run out of food or money. The promises of God are real; He does not change His mind like we do. He is always the same God, no matter what we may face. I have learned, over the years, that fear comes from a lack of trust in God.

God has an unlimited amount of resources He can tap into, things we have no clue were accessible to us. The thing that I have come to learn about God is that His thinking is not our thinking, and His ways are not our ways. While we are thinking about how to pay the bill, God has already planned for the bill to be paid.

Our thinking is so small in comparison to God's ability; we often think we need the resource when we need the creator of the resource. There have been plenty of times in my life when I had a need, and instead of getting just the need, God met the need and more. So many times, in my life instead of facing fear, I ignored fear as if it would go away; let me tell you right now that it did not go away. You must be intentional about fighting your greatest fears face-to-face.

Chapter 5

Fix Your Focus

It was the first week in June of 2013, and I had spent the last month still recovering from the loss of my mother. The weight of her death had been lifted; however, the place where love once lived had yet to heal. As I sat in my sister's living room, drinking a cold Corona, and staring out the front window, life seemed a bit blurry. Nothing made sense; it seemed as though I was stuck between two different dimensions. One was like a dream state, the other my reality. As I think back, I remember my sister asking me several times throughout the entire process if I wanted to get out of the house and go somewhere, and my response remained unchanged, "NO".

Most of the time, I was either sleeping on her couch or sitting in the living room, drinking, and staring out the window. My world had come crashing down in the blink of an eye, and all I could think about was how life was supposed to go on without the woman whom I thought would outlive me. One thing I learned is that life goes on, regardless of how you see it or how you feel about it.

Nothing gets better until you commit to making the change necessary to move on. To be honest, my mind was not in the right place, which caused my focus to be off. Maybe you've experienced losing a parent, a loved one, or even a close friend.

For me, it came at a time when I really couldn't afford it mentally, physically, or financially.

After moving from Michigan to Tennessee less than two months prior, I was still in the process of getting adjusted from the move, staying with a friend's mom, and starting a new demanding job. With everything being new, it was overwhelming to have such a huge blow come at such an unexpected time. Just imagine your life starting to turn around and suddenly having one day impact your entire life.

I could not eat, sleep, or even hardly work. With all that was going on, my mind felt like Atlanta traffic during peak hours. Little did I know that once I crossed the state line between North Carolina and Tennessee, it would be the last time I would be home for a long time.

Life changed in such a way that when I arrived back in Tennessee, I was a completely different person mentally and spiritually. The broken pieces were well concealed, and I buried every part of the hurt, pain, and loss into the deepest parts of my inner being. Somewhere deep inside, I knew that I would have to face these issues again, but my main goal at the time was to get back to a normal life.

Upon arriving back, I received a phone call on that Sunday evening from my employer that I no longer was a good fit for the company. Completely frustrated and blindsided again, my first reaction was: what would be my next move? With a blurry vision, my focus shifted to another opportunity that came up in the midst of all the madness going on in my life. Two days later, a club owner called. He wanted to discuss the chance to be the exclusive photographer for his new after-hours club. At the time, it seemed like the best move to make. Without consulting God, I dove headfirst into what I thought was the best move.

Things started slowly, and money was slow but steady. And then one day, things broke out, and the $150 weekend nights turned into $1500 every Friday and Saturday. The money was great; however, in the process, I lost myself in the situation, which was not the environment I needed fresh off such a devastating loss. What started as just casual drinking turned into an every weekend thing, and I had slowly become a part of the crowd. At one point, I forgot I had a job as a photographer and began to party my life away.

The pain I had buried had slowly started to creep back up into my everyday life. With all the parties and the grind, I was pushed to a point where I had a nervous breakdown. My body had been pushed beyond its limit, and so many factors played a huge role in the breakdown that pinpointing one particular thing would be difficult. The issue that stands out above all other issues was simple: my focus was not intentional, and I had no accountability partner. It was clearly my lifestyle and actions that did not line up with the vision that was in my original plan.

Sometimes God will allow a series of events to happen not as punishment but to get our attention. In my experience, it is a clear sign that the road that is being traveled is one with a dangerous end. It is up to you to recognize that he is guiding you back on the right path. God is the navigator of your life, and the more you travel the course that has been set before you, the more you learn to trust His process. There is a scripture that illustrates the focus we must have and explains with detail why we must stay focused.

In Philippians chapter 3, verses 15-21 (MSG), it reads: "*So let's keep focused on that goal, those of us who want everything God has for us. If any of you have something else in mind, something less than total commitment, God will clear your blurred vision - you'll see it yet! Now that we're on the right track, let's stay on it. Stick with me, friends. Keep track of those you see running this same course, headed for this same goal. There are many out there taking other paths, choosing other goals, and trying to get you to go along with them. I've warned you of them many times; sadly, I have to do it again. All they want is easy street. They hate Christ's Cross. But Easy Street is a dead-end street. Those who live there make their bellies their gods; belches are their praise; all they can think of is their appetites. But there's far more to life for us. We're citizens of high heaven! We await the Savior, the Master, and our Lord, Jesus Christ. He will transform our bodies to be like his, glorious. He'll make us beautiful and whole with the same powerful skill by which he is putting everything, as it should be, under and around him.*"

This version of the scripture is clear and concrete about the purpose of being focused. It is important that we are surrounded by the right people, those that are headed in the same direction with the same common goals. Too many times in my own life, my heart and intentions were good; however, the people that I was surrounded by had no vision and were stuck on easy street.

You will learn quickly that not everyone has your best interests at heart. People care only about how they can benefit from your success. This is why it is so vital for us to pray for wisdom and discernment to know exactly what God's will is for our life.

Today, there are thousands of different get-rich-quick schemes that seem like the quickest way to reach success. Let me point out that nothing that happens fast lasts long; it usually lasts for a brief period and then turns into a dead-end street.

For example, have you ever been so hungry that you just wanted something to satisfy your hunger? In your mind, you thought of something quick and inexpensive; however, once you ate that quick and cheap meal, you were right back hungry. Fast food was never intended to satisfy your hunger but rather to be a temporary quick fix.

When you think about a homemade meal, there is a preparation process that must take place. The beautiful thing about waiting for this amazing meal is that the food is prepared with love. Each part of the meal is carefully prepared with the right measurements, the best seasonings, and cooked at the right temperature. Not only will the meal satisfy your hunger, but it will also cause you to be full longer.

It is truly the same principle with God; our temporary fast-food solutions barely satisfy our needs, and as a result, we are back in the hungry position we started from.

When we attempt to take action into our hands, we are merely saying that we can prepare life's full-course meal better than the Great I Am. The most awkward thing to understand during trials and tribulations is that no matter what circumstances we face, God has the final say. Although it is easier said than done, we have to seek his word for the answers to the issues we face. The problem you often face when you lean to your understanding is that you don't see the end; your focus is on the immediate threat.

The solution that God has for whatever you face is far better than anything that you could imagine. Everything that God orchestrates always has your best interest not only in the end but also along the way. Through all the pain, hurt, and frustration,

God is waiting for you to surrender; his plans are for your good. From my own experience, I would become so frustrated with my limited view of the situation that, by the time I put it in God's hands, it felt like punishment.

As we refer to the scripture it reads: *"Keep track of those you see running this same course, headed for this same goal. There are many out there taking other paths, choosing other goals, and trying to get you to go along with them. I've warned you of them many times; sadly, I have to do it again. All they want is easy street. They hate Christ's Cross. But easy street is a dead-end street. Those who live there make their bellies their gods; belches are their praise; all they can think of is their appetites. But there's far more to life for us."*

My initial reaction while studying this scripture was: who are these people, what do they look like, and how will I know who they are? The answer is beyond clear; the very people that this scripture is referring to are the people you are around. Everyone in your immediate circle reflects you, and it is time you step back and do a circle check. There is an old saying that if you hang around 9 wealthy people, you are bound to be the 10th, but if you hang around 9 broke people, guess what…. Yep, you will most likely be the 10th.

The people you are around the most play a huge role in your life because they have the power of influence. Influence is priceless. If you and your friends planned a night out and you wanted to bail, they would know what to say to motivate you to go out. See, the issue we must face is that everyone that seems to be headed in the direction you are going does not mean that they are committed as you. You need people who will make sacrifices. They shouldn't want easy access. They must want to work nonstop to achieve the set goals. The key to having relentless focus is to seek God's will for your life in all things big or small. When God is the center of your world nothing is ever out of alignment and even your bad days work in your favor.

Chapter 6

Cracked But Not Broken

Life will bring high-pressure situations, hardships, and setbacks. No matter what we face, there is a plan for our lives, and God will always bring us through. It is amazing that our breakthrough often comes at our breaking point. There are several different translations of the Bible, some with old and modern-day languages. In 2 Corinthians chapter 4 verse 8, there is a scripture that when read in The Voice (VOICE version) gives an in-depth look at an old passage with a modern-day eye: *"We are cracked and chipped from our afflictions on all sides, but we are not crushed by them. We are bewildered at times, but we do not give in to despair."*

When I was first led to this scripture, the various translations did not elaborate on its context as I would like. After researching further, I came across this jewel, and it has a lot of vital content that is important to the process of our victory.

How many times as a child did you or your siblings knock over your parents' vase or flowerpot? Even if the vase or pot were chipped, it could be repaired with strong glue or adhesive. Your punishment was severe in comparison to how easy it was to fix the cracked or chipped vessel. The pain that you caused your parents at the time was partly because the vase or flowerpot was valuable and because they had repeatedly warned you several times about playing in an area where this prized possession was placed.

As parents, we love our children, but unfortunately, discipline is needed in certain situations. This is exactly how God works with us; we are His children, and we often end up in areas or on paths that may cause damage to our purpose. Our Heavenly Father, who sits high and looks low, is always watching our every move, eager to repair our cracked and chipped pieces.

The key to the healing process is not to continue to pick at the wounded area. Our disobedience often leads us into situations where we feel hurt, disappointed, or ashamed. Even in our folly, He still accepts and loves us.

A lot of the situations we find ourselves in were created by preconceived thoughts which we felt were best. Without consulting God first, we leap into action with our own understanding and feel let down when we do not yield the results we often hope for.

Although we may not understand the process, it is in our best interest to allow God to have full control. Let me be the first to tell you that if you genuinely want victory in every area of your life, you must make great sacrifices. It is a painful process; when Christ said, "Pick up your cross and follow me," my question to you is where did you think you were going?

There is a spiritual exchange that must take place, and part of that process will require parts of our old self to be cracked, chipped, afflicted, crushed, and bewildered. It may sound insane; however, think about the great people in biblical history and the enormous odds they met for their breakthroughs.

Take a few moments and think about your life and the enormous odds you have overcame to get to the point where you are now.

Maybe, it was your childhood, a failed marriage, or even a car accident that threatened to take your life. You are still reaching, achieving, and breaking new barriers as you move forward. No matter what happens in life, you must not allow the enemy to trick you into feeling despair; do not lose your focus.

Will circumstances arise that will seem out of your control? Yes. Will you face setbacks? Yes. Will you lose friends and family members along the way? Yes. It is all part of the process; we have all been uniquely created and all have a valuable role to play in God's plan.

Identifying your role and how you fit into this intricate plan is about your relationship with God. Every day that we have been blessed to see is another opportunity to seek God with our whole being and pursue our purpose. Give God all your cracked pieces and allow Him to restore every area of your life where you may feel crushed. The beautiful thing about the scripture that I relate to is that if you have hope, your faith still has fight. When you lose hope your faith becomes weakened, and you start to feel undeserving of God's best for your life.

We have all suffered losses and setbacks; the difference in most of our lives is we know how to dust ourselves off and get back into the fight. Some of life's greatest lessons come from watching little kids play and run around bouncing off walls and running into each other, living with no regrets. Oftentimes kids will run into each other, fall, and bounce right back up.

God is right there with you every time you fall; every time you stumble, His grace, mercy, and favor are there to help you get right back up. You may be experiencing some unpleasant situations even as you read this chapter, just know that you are not broken and that there is nothing that can stop you if you would just give whatever it is you are facing to God.

Pick yourself up, go outside for a walk, watch a movie, and spend some time with those you love; whatever you do, GET UP! Do not become idle in your thinking or actions; the things that we fear the most are the things we must run towards with confidence.

Chapter 7

Overcoming The Past

No one runs forward while looking back; that sounds like a recipe for disaster. Growing up in Salisbury, a small city in North Carolina, everyone knew everyone, and as a young teen, it was hard to get away with anything. There was nowhere you could go where someone's family did not know you. At the time, it seemed irritating; however, as I look back, I realize that it was for my good.

Luckily, I survived the storms of life but not before learning some tough lessons along the way. No one is proud of their past, and we all have made some questionable decisions. The beautiful thing about time is that it always moves forward, and for those of us who are blessed enough to see the error of our ways, second chances are available.

Earlier in Chapter 5, we discussed "Fix Your Focus" and the importance of running in the right direction with others who are going toward the same mark that you have been called to. As a young teen, I was witty, hardheaded, and defiant. My dad spent most of his time hanging in the streets while my mother worked as a supervisor for a local college and attended church. She provided us with her best; with no father figure in my life, I was attracted to the street life that most of my friends were already living.

As a teen, I was eager to get out into the streets and experience the life that all my friends were living; it was fast money and came with a lot of perks. Later in life, those so-called friends would set me up and leave me hanging, only to face the consequences of my own decisions.

Most of my young adult years were spent running away from home, in foster care, group homes, and juvenile detention centers across the state. My life was out of control, and my mother had done all she could to keep me from the grasp of the enemy and my poor decisions. The only thing left was her faith, hope, prayers, and belief that God had a plan and was watching over me.

Before I was eighteen, I found myself locked in a jail cell one minute and, over time, headed to prison the next. As I stared out the window of a damp, cold prison van, it dawned on me that no one could save me. Not my mother, sister, or grandparents. No one.

It was all my fault, no one to blame, and no one to point the finger at; it was all on me, and it was time to grow up. Over the next few years, from 1999 to 2003, every fall I would be headed to jail or prison like clockwork. It had become so familiar to my family that no one expected my presence during the fall events or even Christmas.

It was in 2003 when I was released from prison after serving time for a probation violation, which would change my life forever. The prison gates started to slide back, an older gentleman named Slim called my name from the basketball court, "Remember our talk, change starts with you, it's up to you, your kids need you don't look back, don't be another number."

As I approached the car, my mother jumped out to give me a hug, and it was a moment I would never forget. While riding in my mother's gray Dodge Neon, my mother asked me what seemed like a million questions. I could barely think or even answer one of her questions because Slim's voice was still ringing in my head.

As I looked over at my mother's mouth, it seemed as if everything was in slow motion; her mouth was moving, but her voice seemed muffled. The trees looked different. The air felt colder. Life felt different. I looked out the window, wondering how to change my life this time. Life doesn't just happen; our choices and decisions impact how the story plays out.

It had taken me way too long to understand, and a lot of the situations I found myself in were solely based on my decisions. At the age of 26, I was married with one beautiful daughter who lived with her grandmother and a handsome son who lived with his mother and me. Life seemed to be turning around, and things were starting to look up. It was about making the best of what had happened while looking forward to the future.

Marriage was good for the time it lasted, but I had some dark secrets that would ultimately become my nightmare and almost cost me my life. The problem with love for me at the time was I never really knew what it was; in my mind, love was only for squares and parents.

Most of my life was spent in the streets with older men who taught me about fast money, guns, and how to manipulate women. That style of thinking and behavior lived inside of me and was the cause of my marriage failure. As I lay in the hospital with over 32 stab wounds and a near-death experience, it all started making sense what was wrong in my life?

Change was needed, and this was my last warning before my second chances had run their course. It was at this place in my life that I realized nothing was going to change unless I was intentional about the change that was needed. The change I needed started in my mind and through my behaviors and actions; I was determined to get away from what was familiar to me. It was time for real change, and it started with going to college over 800 miles away in Tennessee.

Everyone wasn't on board with my decision; my mother thought it was a bad idea because I didn't know anyone. My sister was the only one who believed in me. My friends thought it was the wrong choice. But it was my life and my choice. God is a second, third, and fourth-chance kind of God; it's up to us to identify when we must surrender and let him have his way.

Shortly after arriving in Tennessee, I realized that I was a step away from a new life, and the possibilities were endless. Everything happens for a reason. God's timing is perfect. At 30, I was a freshman in college and my only focus was to graduate.

Some of the people I met had children, while others had come from broken homes and would be the first in their families to graduate from college. God connected me to people who wanted to see me excel. They barely knew me, but their prayers and encouragement pushed me to go farther in my studies and work. No matter how far you go in life and no matter how alone you may feel, God always gives you what you need on your journey.

Two young ladies at the school, Barbara, and Joann, saw something different in me. They inspired me to achieve more and to keep going, no matter what. It was a fire burning inside of me, and not only did I feel it, but other people could also see it. Today, those wonderful ladies still contact me sometimes to see how I am doing.

Two years later, I found myself preparing to walk across a stage that so many others had walked across long before me. As I sat, eager to be called to the stage, my mind shifted back to where I started. It took only a change in my thinking to get here. It was my failure to realize that pointing the finger and making excuses only affected my life.

What other people were doing had nothing to do with my actions, and if I wanted something different in life, I had to face my own poor decisions and responsibilities. For the first time in my life, I felt empowered and accomplished as my mom, dad, classmates, and friends watched as I humbly walked across the stage. It was truly God's grace that had forwarded me a second chance in life.

We all have a past; what we often fail to realize is that our past can never be relived. Our experiences give us life lessons that we will draw from later in life to help us make better decisions. Although we may face hardships, setbacks, and calamities, God will never leave or forsake us no matter what giants we may face along the way.

No one can change his or her past; however, what he or she can do is start where they are and focus on the root of their problems. Nothing in life is easy; one of the first things I had to do was find out what stage of life I was in. Overcoming the past is about knowing what stage of life you are in.

The stages of life have nothing to do with your age, ability, talent, gifts, or experiences. Leave nothing to regret, make every single move count, leave nothing on the table, be responsible and accountable to yourself. Look around you and realize that we are living in a critical time, and no one is promised tomorrow. Make decisions that better not only yourself but also those around you.

As believers in Christ, we must walk by faith, not by sight. Our walk can influence those facing issues we once faced. Our past experiences are key indicators to those who may be watching that you can overcome anything that you are facing.

Too often, we make sacrifices for material things not realizing that none of those things matter. What if we took that same mentality and applied it to our goals and dreams? Do not give up, I believe you can make the change needed to overcome your past.

Chapter 8

The Power of No

In the last two weeks, how many times have you been influenced by the thoughts, ideas, or actions of someone else? Today, the power of social media has grown, and we have been connected virtually through technology. We have the power to access other people in different countries around the globe right at our fingertips. We allow outside influences to impact and affect our thoughts, feelings, emotions, and decisions without saying a word.

Everything that you view with your eyes is being registered in your mind. We silently read funny memes and then laugh out loud. We read inspirational quotes and become inspired by words we never heard. We watch violent videos in the comfort of our own homes and become either emotionally attached or detached from the scenes that unfold before our eyes.

The power of no gives us the ability to have a filter system in place for exactly what we allow into our lives. We live in a microwave world where everything is produced at a high rate: our food, clothes, cars, television programming, and even our thinking. The power of no eliminates our microwave thinking and calls for sound reasoning, no matter how dire the situation.

Success starts with the power of no. You have to take an honest assessment of your life and identify the areas that need the power of no. It could be your financial spending, your circle of friends, or even bad habits that cause you to make poor decisions. You must begin to ask yourself how much power and influence have you given to things, people, and places that either distract you or cause you to make poor choices.

The power of no will separate the people, places, and things that are not encouraging you to reach your fullest potential. Real change happens when you make decisions and sacrifices that better you. We often fall victim to seeing other people's success not knowing the layers of struggle that took place.

Everyone's success is different, and struggling is not a place that anyone asks to be; it is a transitional place that very few people exit because they lack the power of no. Life for me changed completely when I started making better decisions. One of the key things that helped me understand what I wanted was learning to be alright with people not agreeing with my decisions.

Your best life is right around the corner. It is never too late to accomplish anything; all it takes is making better decisions and using the power of no. Understanding that saying yes to every situation that arises will stretch you thin and limit your productivity.

People pleasing has never accomplished anything; you will learn that even after you have completed your commitment to people, someone will still want more or be completely unsatisfied. One of the toughest lessons I have learned in life is that you can never satisfy everybody; someone will always be unhappy. I have attempted to please everyone too many times and ended up frustrated, broke, and tired. It never failed; as soon as one person seemed pleased, another person would complain about how unhappy they were and how I didn't care about their feelings.

We have given too much time and effort into convincing people we care about them when they could care less about us. The truth of the matter is that the more accessible yes is in our vocabulary, the more likely we are not willing to use the power of no.

We have become mentally and emotionally attached to situations and people that intentionally hinder our growth. We feel ashamed or self-conscious about turning them down, and we place ourselves in their shoes and sympathize with whatever it is they're going through.

Believe me, I can relate. One Sunday, I was in the grocery store shopping with my youngest son, and we were enjoying a funny moment when out of nowhere, a man came from behind me. A bit startled and caught off guard, the man knowingly jumped into a story about him and his wife running out of gas and being on their way back to Memphis, with kids in the car, and the list just seemed to go on.

After all that, I just wanted him to get going so I could go back to enjoying my quality time with my son. The man asked for a few dollars, which turned into $20, and as my son looked on, the whole situation became more of a performance. For a moment, I will say if it wasn't for my son being there, I would have completely said no; however, my son had those puppy eyes, and it just ruined my awesome no.

Moving right along, I gave the man the $20, and he said, "God bless you," and thanked me as he walked off. At that moment, I felt good; my good deed had been done, and my son and I continued to shop. As we made our way to the checkout, I glanced over at the deli area and noticed the man buying food, which set my soul on fire.

Instead of approaching the guy, I just mumbled a few choice words under my breath and proceeded to checkout. In my mind, as I scanned groceries, it made me realize that even with my son there, I could have easily used my power of no. As I looked back on the whole situation, a few factors played a role in my decision. The first thing I noticed was being caught off guard, then the long-drawn-out story while I was still recovering mentally from a sudden startle. My son was watching my every move, seeing how daddy would handle the situation.

Ladies and gentlemen, I had just been beaten, no way around it. At no point during the entire situation did I have total control of the situation or my thinking; therefore, it made it difficult to use the power of no when everything was pointing to yes. Unfortunately, that would not be the last time I would have an encounter with someone with a story and a need.

It has happened to people all over the world; no matter where you are from, you have experienced a panhandler asking you for money and have either used the power of no or accessed your yes by giving. Even in such a simple illustration, we see that in a split second, two different outcomes can happen based solely on our accessibility to yes and the power to say no. What makes us say no to people in need and yes to family members or friends who may be facing a comparable situation?

In most cases, we do not relate to the stranger who may be facing tough times; however, we are kin to the family member or friend who may be. Being kin does not necessarily mean by relationship;

it could be the situation that makes you relatable. There are things going on in your life right now that have allowed your yes to put you in an uncomfortable position. Whatever your "it" is may be causing you discomfort.

It may be time to look at what you have been giving your yes to and start looking at the power of no. Maybe it is your spending, hanging out with friends, shopping, or doing more for others than for yourself. Whatever your "it" is may be the reason why you are not seeing any progress.

Take a good look at the areas in your life where you feel discomfort and be honest with yourself. Ask yourself, is it worth it? How is my "it" helping me get closer to where I want to be? Don't miss it; look very closely. It doesn't have to be a thing; your "it" could be a person, your "it" could be a habit, your "it" could be a family member that is pulling on you. Your "it" is the reason why you're unhappy.

We are often influenced by our emotions and not God's word. We feel compassionate about others, and there is nothing wrong with that; however, we must consult God in all we do. Just because it feels like the right thing to do does not mean God is in it.

The power of no deals with consulting God before we do things that are questionable; we are followers of Christ, and our aim is to imitate him while here on earth. Some things are not complicated; we make them complicated by overthinking and not being led by the spirit.

From my own experience, I have learned that if I can find it in the word of God, then it is a promise, and it takes faith to believe that it shall come to pass. A notable example would be my neighbor suddenly knocking on the door and asking if I knew anyone that he could borrow $45 to get his truck fixed. He goes on to say if I did not know anyone, would I be able to help?

At that very moment, I was tossed into a situation where it was a matter of faith. Here I am with 45 dollars, with a bill coming up in the next three days, and a neighbor in need. Instead of offering the money right away, I felt it was best to tell my neighbor that I would see what I could do and get back to him on the situation.

First, I went to God, prayed about the situation, and asked for guidance; I needed the money as much as he did. The situation seemed dire, and I was not getting an answer fast enough from God, in an act of wisdom before foolishness, I called an aunt who lived in Maryland to get more understanding.

Deep in my heart, I felt as if I knew exactly what to do, but for some reason, I needed confirmation. About 20 minutes passed, and my aunt called my phone, with little hesitation, I explained to her the situation and how I felt led to take this leap of faith. Her exact words were, "Let's pray." After we prayed, she had a business call, and we hung up the phone. Still not convinced, I looked up scriptures about neighbors, and lo and behold, there it was.

As I read the scripture, the words penetrated my flesh and entered my soul. The scripture was Proverbs 3:28, and it read, *"Do not say to your neighbor, 'Go and come back and tomorrow I will give it,' when you have it with you."* It was right in my face, plain as day. After praying, consulting, and seeking the scripture, it was right there the whole time.

Not so much of the scripture; the scripture has always been there, but the opportunity to live out the word of God right in front of my very eyes. In my heart, I knew what to do when the neighbor first knocked, so what caused me to seek the answers when the answer was in me the whole time?

To this day, it was a matter of overthinking an opportunity to help someone in need when I had a need as well. The amazing part that I reflect on in this situation is that if we trust God to provide all our needs, what do we have to fear by helping others? The power of no can be simple, or complex based solely on our thinking. We know what is right in our hearts; however, we often miss opportunities for God to use us or elevate our faith to new levels based on our own needs.

A long-time friend and pastor that I have known since 2009 gave me some sound advice when I told him the story. He said that we are not babies in Christ or in spirit, and there are certain things you just do because it is in His Word and will.

Chapter 9

Unexpected Blessings

As far back as I can remember, God has always protected and provided for me, even when I didn't deserve it. There have been times when I was right, and there have been times when I was simply wrong. God's love never changed; His blessings still found me, not because of my good or bad deeds, but because His mercy and favor endure forever. It was nothing I did in my own ability; unexpected blessings often happen to us through the prayers of our family, church members, and even perfect strangers.

There have been a lot of prayers that have been prayed on my behalf. When you have a mother and grandmother who start and end their day with God first, you can expect more than just prayers. There may be some laying of hands and olive oil slapped on your forehead and face. (lol, but seriously)

Unexpected blessings can be found throughout the Bible in various stories where people were going about their normal lives and received a blessing. In my own life, there have been countless encounters and experiences of unexpected blessings.

In James chapter 1, verse 17, it is written, *"Every good and perfect gift is from above, coming down from the Father of heavenly lights, who does not change like shifting shadows."* We are not always deserving of the good and perfect gifts; however, God is sovereign. Unlike our earthly caretakers here on earth, God will not forget or fail to provide for our needs. His timing is nothing like our time, and though we may feel it is an immediate need, God's timing is always perfect.

Perfect gifts are not only unexpected; they also come at a time when we least expect them. What better feeling is it than to receive an unexpected gift? These special moments from family, loved ones, friends, a spouse, or even our kids send shockwaves of joy through our hearts. It is the idea that the giver of the gift had us on their mind.

During the last five years, I have experienced these unexpected encounters during the highs in my life as well as the lows. Every experience will be different. They come when you have reached your end or learned a lesson during great distress. Faith is the substance of things hoped for, not things that are seen.

Breakthroughs and miracles require our faith to believe that it shall be. Unexpected blessings require nothing; these blessings are like grace and salvation; you cannot earn them; they have already been awarded and are a part of our acceptance of Jesus Christ. In all we do in life, it is about growth and living the life that we have been called to live. You have been called to carry your cross, and as I mentioned earlier, you don't understand what the journey consists of until you are knee-deep in the battle.

As a believer and follower of Christ, you will suffer as our Savior did. We live in a cruel and unruly world where the enemy is the ruler. You will be tested, mocked, talked about, lied on, and shamed by the world during this life. In every way that Christ was mistreated, you shall experience the same or similar treatment. The prize we shall receive in the end will be a great reward: to have eternal life; there is nothing that can compare.

Many have been called to carry out this great task, but only a few will accept the call. Suffering is part of the process; it is not a lifestyle that anyone initially signs up for; however, just like a school test, how can we know about our level of faith if we are not tested?

Some will choose the easiest path, and others the less traveled one. Unexpected things happen in everyday life, unexplainable things: the child that falls while crossing the street as a car fails to stop and misses hitting the child by seconds or even minutes. The car wreck that nearly took your life, or a family member's life, but somehow you survived and came out with little to no scratches.

Encounters like this and many others cannot be put into words to describe the outcome, which we often call a blessing. In that moment, we become internally grateful and often feel overwhelmed. There are hundreds of thousands of stories around the globe that people have shared publicly that testify to the goodness of an unexpected blessing.

These stories inspire us to believe that God is real and that there is hope for us wherever we may find ourselves in life. Right now, at this very moment, someone needs an unexpected blessing, and sometimes God will use other resources to fill the void that we may need. Knowing that God is the source, then we should know and understand that He works through all that He has created. The process or the way things get done may change, but God remains the same no matter what we may encounter along the way.

Growing up, my grandmother would say trivial things that did not make sense at the time, but as I grew older and life happened, I started seeing those very things she spoke of happen in my own life. One of my favorite sayings she had was *"People may not always be able to give you money, but they will give you food."* As life went on, I found that her advice would manifest in situations in my life where money was not my immediate need.

As a single parent, it was food that was needed more than money, and just like she said, people were able to bless me. We are all brothers and sisters in Christ, and our compassion for each other is often displayed through our actions.

In Luke chapter 6, verse 38, we find a scripture that many recite without honestly believing the impact that this scripture provides. It reads, *"Give, and you will receive. Your gift will return to you in full – pressed down, shaken together to make room for more, running over, and poured into your lap. The amount you give will determine the amount you get back"* (NLT).

In verse 38 there is no period or limitation on when you will receive this amazing gift. This is a promise; there are five promises in this scripture the first promise is give and you shall receive; promise number two says your gift will return to you in full. Promise three simply says pressed down; promise four states shaken together to make more room.

Promise five says running over and poured into your lap. This entire scripture in Luke chapter 6, verse 38, is symbolic of grace; you cannot outgive God. The grace displayed in the verse is infinite and has no time attached to it. It truly is a promise that what you give and how much you give will be returned in overflow.

Not only is this scripture literal, but it never specifies what specific thing has been given. It could be your time, insight, wisdom, food, or money. Whatever you give out of what you have will be returned to you. It simply says the measure that you give will determine the measure you get back.

Unexpected blessings come at a time when we need them and often come with abundance according to what your giving has been. This is certainly not a method to get blessings to fall out of the sky but a perspective to see when you are giving. God judges the heart of man. It does not matter if you had a million dollars and donated $50,000, if you had a grudge in your heart; then that giving meant nothing.

Your heart determines the measure as well; faith takes believing that out of your giving, God will supply your needs. One of the great examples of an unexpected blessing can be found in 1 Kings chapter 17, verses 10 through 16 when a widow had only enough bread and oil for her and her son.

Elijah the Prophet asked her for some bread, and when she told him she only had enough to eat with her son and die, he told her not to be afraid and gave her specific instructions to fix his bread first and that her flour and oil would not run out.

Two things stand out in this story: one is when we are obedient, God will honor our obedience. Also, when we are willing to give out of the little we have and trust that God is our source, whatever we give, God will always bless us beyond our giving.

The widow had no idea that she was in line for an unexpected blessing; even in her response, she says, "And surely as the Lord your God lives," meaning God knows I want to help; however, all that I have is enough for me and my son.

Do you know what it takes to give out of an area in your life where you do not even have enough? This was her plea; how can I give you something that I do not even have enough of? In her mind, her thoughts were if I give you what we have, then what shall we eat? Her only intention was to feed her son, herself, and die. What makes this story so relatable is the fact that she was a single parent who had hit a rough spot and was down to her last.

In my mind, I wonder how many other single parents have been in a similar situation and wanted to help someone in need, but the thought of going without caused them to miss an unexpected blessing. There have been several times in my life when we only had enough food to last for a few days, and instead of eating, I prepared a meal for my son and went without.

Even in those times, God provided a way; a friend or a neighbor would offer food or money to get food. God is always watching our heart; He knows exactly what we stand in need of and is often waiting for us to ask for His guidance and help.

Over the years, I have honestly learned that God is not like man; He will not lie or forsake you. Although things do not go the way that I think they should go, His timing is perfect. God's plan for our lives is far better than anything we can imagine, and we must learn to trust His ways more than our own. Just like the manna God provided for the Israelites in their time of need, we can trust He will do the same for us.

We often lean on our understanding when situations come into our lives that we do not understand. We often rush to fix one issue, and new ones arise. God's system is fail-proof.

Chapter 10

No Turnovers

In every game of sports, the key aspect of every victory is teamwork. Every sports fanatic hates to see their team turn the ball over. One of the most memorable moments in sports happened when the Tennessee Titans were on the goal line. They had four opportunities to score the winning touchdown and win the Super Bowl against the Pittsburgh Steelers. It was 4th and 1 yard to go, which meant they were only 1 yard away from winning the biggest championship game in Titan history.

They only needed to break the plane of the goal line to score, and after three previous attempts, a fourth attempt did not produce a score. Can you imagine practicing in the offseason, putting in all the hard work, and making it to the championship game only to lose? Every player's goal in any sport is to win a championship.

In every sport, there is a story of some team, player, or person that beat every opponent only to get to the championship game or race and fall short. It seems heartbreaking to work so hard to see the victory go right into the opponent's hands. Over the years, I have learned that when you go back and watch the entire event, somewhere during the game, fight, race, or match, there was a turning point.

Every sport is different; however, at the end of the day, a win is a win, and a loss is a loss. Winning is about making the right decisions at the right time, outscoring the other opponent, or leading most of the race for all those racing fans. From a defensive standpoint, the strategy is simple: keep your opponent from scoring or getting in the lead.

One of the major keys to any victory in sports is avoiding turnovers, especially in sports where a ball is involved. Here is the biggest issue with turnovers: you give the ball to the other team and fail to score on your possession. When you give the ball to the other team, you give them your opportunity to score.

Just like sports, as followers of Christ, we are on a team and our opponent, the enemy, is looking to take away our possessions, which are the blessings of God. If we are not careful with our blessings, they could become bad possessions and then we forfeit them to the enemy by default.

When we look in the Bible at John chapter 10, verse 10, there is a scripture that warns us about our enemy, and it reads, *"The thief approaches with malicious intent, looking to steal, slaughter, and destroy; I came to give life with joy and abundance."* In every sport, your opponent's intent is to get the victory by any means needed. In basketball, they will grab jerseys; in football, they will grab facemasks; in boxing, low blows; and in racing, special parts.

That is exactly what the enemy wants to do to those who have accepted the calling to pick up their cross and follow Jesus. The enemy will do everything in his power to steal and destroy you, and it is why we must be very alert in how we handle our blessings. In the last chapter, we spoke about unexpected blessings, and the enemy hates more than anything for us to get those types of blessings.

Too many times I have experienced or witnessed a family member or friend receive an unexpected blessing, and the enemy will use every device in his power and under the sun to rip it away from them. He will use pride, selfishness, old debts, bad habits, and even loved ones to force you to turn over your blessings.

There is nothing more frustrating than to have a blessing slip right through your fingers. It is like a quarterback throwing the perfect pass, and you drop the pass, or it goes through your hands. Too many times in my life, I have been in a prime position to receive a blessing, and I allowed the enemy to steal it.

There have even been times when God blessed me, and I mismanaged the blessing and turned it over to the enemy through my actions. Job was highly favored by God. But God allowed the enemy to destroy everything he owned. Nothing happens by accident; we either cause it through our actions and decisions or God allows it to happen.

Let's be honest for a second; God will not force anything on us; it is up to us to choose; we have the power of free will. We can choose what we want: life or death the power is in every decision.

Have you ever watched a football or basketball game, and your favorite team just kept taking bad shots or throwing interceptions? How did it make you feel? Just imagine how the coaches and other teammates felt as they dropped their heads in disgust at yet another turnover.

The game of life cannot be won unless we take care of the Rock. God is our Father, and Jesus is the Rock. In our time of need, God sends us blessings, and how we handle those blessings determines if God can trust us with even greater. The issue that we often run into is that we mismanage the blessings that God has already blessed us with.

As a parent, do you keep rewarding your child for poor behavior or bad grades? So why do we feel entitled to keep receiving from God when we are disobedient? The enemy laughs at us when we make bad decisions and poor choices because he knows that we have given him permission to enter our huddle and steal our plays.

We must become mindful of how our thoughts, actions, and habits are aligned in our daily walk. Nobody wants to work all through life and get to the finish line and be denied access. As we look back at John chapter 10, verse 10, we see that we have already been awarded the victory through the promise of Jesus Christ. It says, *"I came to give life with joy and abundance."* When we look at the whole verse, we see that the enemy has a job to do, and we have been given a reward if we are faithful. The reward is life with joy and abundance; this is exactly what the enemy wants to steal, kill, and destroy.

We must revisit and reference 1 Peter chapter 5:8, which says, *"Most importantly, be disciplined and stay on guard. Your enemy the devil is prowling around outside like a roaring lion, just waiting and hoping for the chance to devour someone."* As the game of life moves forward, the journey and the battles get tougher, but our opponent stays the same. The enemy may adjust his style of play, but he will always be the opposition; he has malicious intent to slaughter anyone that has been rewarded the promise.

As followers of Christ, we must stay alert and ready for war at any given time. There is nothing greater than to finish the race and hear, "*Well done, good and faithful servant.*" Turnovers cost points, and in our case, it could very well be the difference in our final position in eternity. Through Christ's death, we have been given power and authority to take back what the enemy has stolen from us, but it is up to us to use that power. Do not allow the vices of the enemy to cause you to fumble the promises of your life away. Hold tight and proceed with the intent to put the enemy back in his place on purpose.

Chapter 11

Call A Timeout

Have you ever felt that your life was heading in the wrong direction? It felt as if some unstoppable force was pushing you into the outer realms of life. No matter what you did right, life kept driving you in the wrong direction. There are numerous times that I can remember in my life when it felt like some unmovable force was fighting against my every move.

In football, there is a unit on the team called a special team, which has a punter who punts the ball to the opposing team. The job of the punter's teammates is to protect the ball from being blocked. Their secondary job is to run down the field as fast as possible and tackle whoever has the ball. The opposing team will have 11 players on their team; one of those players specializes in returning the ball and will be the fastest player on the team.

As soon as the punter punts the ball, the two outside players are doing everything in their power to get to the receiver of the ball the fastest. Meanwhile, the two players assigned to the outside players are trying to push them out of bounds and keep them out of the play. After explaining all of that, I feel a bit tired; however, let's keep going, stay with me. There will be some pushing and shoving going on as the outside players get closer to the man with the ball.

In all my years of watching football, there has hardly been a time when the outside players reach the player with the ball first. Usually, the player with the ball runs straight up the middle or to the outside with two blockers. Sometimes in life, we will be pushed out of bounds by situations, poor choices, and bad decisions; it's life and things happen.

The whistle of life has not been blown, so the play is still alive, and there is still time on the clock. Getting knocked down is part of the game; getting back up after you have been knocked on your backside takes heart. When life gets tough and it starts pushing and shoving you around, sometimes you must call a timeout and regroup. If you were to ask any professional athlete on any platform how hard it is to focus during a game when frustrated, they would tell you it is extremely tough.

Players have been taken out of the game and benched because their frustration started to show up in their performance, which eventually affects the team's performance. It is the same way in life; when we are fatigued, frustrated, or upset, our focus goes away from winning, and our attention gets jammed up in our circumstances.

Speaking from experience, nothing good will happen when you're mentally frustrated; you start to overthink and react out of anger. When you are aligned with your purpose, winning and success will come naturally, and no matter what happens in life, you will always finish strong. One of the key issues that we often face in life is that we tend to perform better when we have help than when we are in a one on-one situation.

For example, in a close football game, a defensive back is in zone coverage. He is playing off the wide receiver because he knows he has help in certain areas of the zone. On the flip side, a man-to-man defense requires the defensive back to cover the wide receiver tightly. If the receiver beats the defensive back off the line and gets behind him, he is open. In football, the defensive back has been burnt.

No matter what life throws your way, you must be relentless in your pursuit of scoring. Notice I used the word scoring because scores are small touchdowns that lead to big wins. Too many times we get cocky and prideful and go for the gusto on the first play, and when we get stopped, we lose a huge amount of confidence. We must learn to play the game of life at the level we are on and learn how to build on small wins.

Here is a notable example of what I mean: as a freshly new college graduate, my ambition and cockiness led me to believe that I would land my dream job and life would be happily ever after. Not only did life push me out of bounds, but I found myself constantly getting knocked down because my focus was on the big wins instead of the small accomplishments.

There is nothing more frustrating than to be gifted and talented but lack the IQ of the game. Many talented college football, basketball, and baseball players were great athletes but lacked the IQ needed to compete at the next level. Going from a collegiate level to a professional level is different, and a lot of players are not successful for that simple reason. One of the differences between the college level and the NFL is there is a 2-minute warning and timeout clock, which allows teams time to adjust.

That 2-minute difference is a major factor considering the score and having the right players on the field in a tight game. Another factor that is important is that in college, the clock stops running after a first down, which gives players and coaches time to make subtle adjustments.

In the NFL, the clock continues to run unless a player runs out of bounds or a pass to another player is incomplete. This small difference is in favor of the college players because it extends the game. Timeouts are important not only in sports but in life because they give us time to adjust how we approach situations we may face. Critical thinking plays a vital role in sports, and having the right personnel on the team determines how the outcome of the game will go.

Coaches and players must be on the same page so that everyone knows exactly the strategy in critical moments when the game is on the line. Who do you have on your team that has a high IQ for the game of life? When you need to call a timeout to make crucial decisions, who do you call? We often discuss options with family, friends, and coworkers. We should always go to God first with any situation we may be facing. Keep in mind that the clock of life does not stop, so every decision that we make will be crucial to the outcome of how we finish.

Having a personal relationship with God is vital to our success as well as our perspective on life. God is the creator of the field on which we play, and who would know better than God what play he has designed for your life? What I have learned is that human thinking is limited, and someone else's perspective may be near-sighted based on their experience. When we take the issues of life to God, not only do we get valuable insight and guidance, but we also get peace of mind.

In moments of tough times and frustration, I often looked for the quickest solution just to get the situation under control. The quickest solutions are not always the best options, especially when the game of life is on the line. Tomorrow is not promised, and if we are blessed to see those new days, we must learn to be intentional about our time here on earth. Making hasty decisions leads to turnovers, and every possession is important.

Social media plays a significant role in our lives because we have instant access to sporting events, concerts, and award shows. We live in a world where everything is in high demand, and we spend less time with God. Learning how to call a timeout allows us to find out if our lives and game plans are lining up with God's will.

Everything that God has planned for your life will happen at the exact time that he has appointed; nothing can change that. God is sitting in the skybox with the best view of the field and can see all the tricks of the enemy. Learning how to trust God, is part of becoming a better player at the game of life.

Chapter 12

Sacrifice To Win

One of the greatest basketball players in NBA history is none other than Michael Jordan. What made Jordan a valuable player was his dedication to the game of basketball; he became the best player he could be. Over his career, Jordan missed 9,000 shots and lost 300 games. He also missed the game-winning shot over 26 times. Yet, he won six NBA championships.

Michael Jordan had a heart and passion not only for the game of basketball but also a desire to win. Jordan was so dedicated to his love for basketball that he once played a game with the flu and still scored 38 points. When Jordan set his mind on winning, he didn't let losing stop him. Another important thing about Jordan was his ability to score at will. At one point in his career, Jordan won three NBA titles back-to-back twice. Then, he decided to pursue his love for baseball, where he first started.

Michael Jordan gave more than his ability to the game of basketball; he gave his heart. What set his game apart from other talented players was his dedication. He was willing to give up his personal life to become a student of the game he loved. To reach your level of greatness, you must find out what it is you have a passion for. You must love your passion with every part of your being; finding your purpose in life starts with your passion. It is something you would do if you were in front of 20,000 fans, or an empty boardroom.

There are countless other great athletes, businesspeople, and women who have dedicated their lives to the love of their fields. Greatness will not happen overnight; you must be willing to give your all to your passion even when no one believes in you. One of the things that I thought made Jordan great was his vision on the court; he played the game with his mind.

When you look at some of his games throughout his career, he made some unbelievable shots from awkward shooting positions. He always understood where he was on the court; his presence to get the shot up to the rim even while being fouled is playing the game with your mind and forcing your body to perform.

People often go on strict diets and discipline their bodies to lift weights and do extreme cardio, not realizing that their bodies are machines. One of the main goals of working out is to get the body in shape and feel good about your health. You must make it a habit at first until it becomes a daily routine. It would be like setting your alarm clock to 4 a.m. to wake you up every morning; eventually, your mind wakes up your body once it has been trained.

We all have good and bad habits that are conducive to our goals and lifestyles. The thing that most of us find difficult to do is break our bad habits; they have become second nature to us and have become part of our normal routine. Michael Jordan became great by making a sound decision about what he wanted to accomplish. He wanted to win championships and to achieve this goal he made sacrifices that would ensure that he was successful.

Jordan spent most of his career in the gym and on the court as a student, player, and leader. While off the court, he used his time to position himself for life after basketball. He played the game of basketball on the court and the game of life off the court. Jordan never lost sight of the vision that he had set, and to become great in every aspect of his life, he was intentional about his actions and decisions.

Success does not just happen; you must do things on purpose; you must make decisions based on where you want to go, not where you are. Most people are not successful for a few reasons. A top reason is their unwillingness to sacrifice. It hinders them from reaching their greatness. Whenever you have a dream, vision, or goal, you must first ask yourself, is it attainable? Am I willing to make the adjustments needed to reach my desired goal?

Having a dream, goal, or vision is a great start because you visualize it before you achieve it. How you create separation and start to make progress towards that goal is like the technique Jordan used to create his shot; you must position yourself to be open. Somewhere out there, a person is pursuing an acting career while someone else's goal is to graduate college; the question that always decides the outcome is what you are willing to sacrifice.

At some point, you must move your feet to create space and opportunity to take a shot at what you have set as your goal. Your shot could have the purest stroke, but it means nothing if you do not have a clear vision of the goal.

How can a quarterback be considered great if he never throws a pass? As a boxer, it is a bit different; your job is to learn the various boxing techniques, skills, and how to move your feet to become a championship fighter. No matter how skilled you become in the training process, you will never know how good you are until you fight in real time. On paper, you could be favored to win the fight but if you get in the ring and don't throw any punches, you are subject to lose.

Sacrifice is about throwing your best punch even if you miss or get knocked down; the key is your decision. Sacrifice is about getting up early and going to bed late; it's about going to the gym and throwing punches when no one is around. It is what drives a student-athlete to shoot jumpers when all their friends are out having a good time. To go from an average player to a great player in any aspect is a process, and it all starts with what you are willing to give up.

One area that separates a good player from a great player is the ability to be flexible. Michael Jordan was a master at adjusting his shot in mid-air, going to or away from the goal. No matter where you find yourself in life, you must be flexible and understand that the path to success is not always straight. If you know what your goal is, it doesn't matter what life throws at you, the harder you work, the closer you'll get.

The way to play the game of life is with your mind and heart; being able to make sound decisions under extreme pressure is an asset. Another key component is taking responsibility for your actions, being accountable for your role in the losses helps you understand how to adjust. There is nothing wrong with celebrating the small victories along the way; the problem that most people have is that they get caught in the twilight zone of short-term accomplishments. No matter how many small victories you get, you should never take your focus off the end goal.

The end goal is the final target you set out to hit in the beginning; everything leading up to that moment is practice. Don't get comfortable or relaxed during the process; use the same amount of focus and energy to accomplish the big task as you did the small task. Right now, there are some things in your life that are bad habits that are hindering you from reaching your goals.

For you, maybe it's watching too much television, shopping, or going out with friends. You must start looking at the big picture; the sacrifices you make today will determine your rewards for tomorrow. To be great at anything in life, you must become a student of the game. Always work toward your goals. The road to winning and success will be a lonely journey; you will lose family and friends.

Do not let what other people are doing distract you from doing what you have set out to do in life. In Chapter 9, we talked about unexpected blessings and how the widow was blessed for being obedient. She followed the exact instructions of Elijah, and it produced an unexpected blessing.

It was her willingness to sacrifice her little portion that caused her to be blessed in abundance. Just imagine if the widow was selfish and decided that feeding herself and her son was more important than this strange man who she had just met. Sometimes it is the little sacrifices we overlook that produce a harvest of results. If Michael Jordan had sat out of the game when he had the flu, he would have never scored 38 points, and the moment would have never made it into his legacy.

In short, sacrifices cause pain but, they often produce the results we hoped for in the end. To grow and become great, we must be willing to learn from our mistakes, forget our old way of thinking, and embrace life's lessons.

Chapter 13

Success for Life

What does success look like to you? Is it a certain amount of wealth, or is it fame? Is it a level of status that you reach? Success comes in all types of shapes and sizes, and it depends solely on the individual more than the idea. A single mother with three kids who graduates from college is a success. The father who rushes from work to make it to his son's first football game is a success. The painter who creates an award-winning masterpiece is a success. The student who turns his C average into a B+ is a success; success is solely based on what a person sets as a goal and achieves.

We live in a judgmental world where people often criticize others for achieving what they define as success. Too many times we allow other people's perspectives of success to determine what our success should look like. We were all born different, and that is what makes the world a beautiful place. Outside of identical twins, no two people are the same. Even when you look at identical twins, there will be something that distinguishes them.

What we eat, how we dress, what we wear, and how we think are all unique. Can you imagine living in a world where everyone looked, talked, dressed, and thought the same? It would be a boring world with no colors, no lines, shapes, or creativity, and everything would be dull. We are always in the rat race of life, always moving and forgetting that we are living in a world created just for us to enjoy. The sights, sounds, colors, intricate designs, and lights are all intended for us to admire and incorporate into our daily activities.

Somehow, we have overlooked these unique aspects and gifts as our mobile devices have become mini remotes to control our minds. It has mysteriously captivated and kidnapped not only our minds but also the minds and focus of kids around the world. We have forgotten how to live and dream. The constant updates of media and entertainment leave us glued to our devices as precious time escapes our hourglass.

We fail to realize that we have given up our own success stories to entertain someone else's. We spend countless hours following the stories of people we have never met, meanwhile neglecting our own lives. Can you imagine what life could be like if we all logged out of social media and allocated our time and resources towards our goals and dreams?

Every single person on the face of this earth has some special gift or talent that either they have yet to discover, or they haven't fully developed. Are we too comfortable with our routine? Have we traded our futures for short-term pleasure? What if we are not living our lives to their fullest potential? At an early age, I realized that I wanted more out of life than what was within my environment. As I grew older, I realized that to get what I wanted, I had to make some tough decisions that not only affected me but also affected my kids, my family, and those I had built relationships with.

One of the toughest decisions that I had to make was whether I would stay in a city where my kids, family, and friends were, or leave and go after my dreams. At the time, the trend in the city was selling drugs, gang activity, violence, and low-paying jobs. It seemed that most people that I knew were comfortable with their position in life and just being alive was a reward rather than a gift. Today, as I look back on my decision to relocate, I realize that the opportunities that I have experienced throughout my career would have never happened if I had listened to the concerns, questions, and fears of other people.

We must be willing to go against what others think is right for us and do what we think is right for us. One of the wonderful things I learned is that people are afraid of change, and nobody wants to pursue its benefits until they see the results it produces. There is something you should know about sacrifice; it is deliberate, painful, and life changing. Most people are not willing to give up their present satisfactions for a fulfilling tomorrow. Death is a painful situation, and losing my mother at that time in my life was tough and a harsh reality check that even after loss life still goes on.

Time doesn't stop, bills will continue to come, and there will still be work to do. There is nothing in my life that I would change; every mistake, every decision, every hardship, and every failure has been part of the process of growth and a requirement of sacrifice. Experience is the best teacher when it comes to the game of life; the more experiences you have, the greater your chances are to escape the pitfalls of your past. Michael Jordan became great on purpose; his journey started long before his legacy became a household name.

Jordan's journey began when he decided in his heart and mind that he wanted his life to be different. Now is the time to adjust; don't wait till it's too late. The game of life has already started, and the clock of the second chance does not exist. Are you putting forth your greatest effort? Are you flexible, can you adjust under pressure? What does success look like to you, and how do you accomplish the goals you have set?

All these questions are important and will have an impact on what your tomorrow will look like. Nothing is promised, and nothing will be given. Leave nothing on the table; take every breath you can, run towards your goals every chance you get, and smile no matter what life may throw your way. Make tough decisions now so that you can live the life you always wanted.

In my heart and mind, I believe the worst death that a person can experience is a death of regret. You gambled life away believing that one day things will be right, it will line up, and you will finally be positioned to take over the world. Sadly, my friend, it will never happen if you are not willing to start your journey where you are. Everything that you ever wanted to do will never happen if you never do it.

Instead of doing what you love, you have been giving your time and attention to the pleasures of life. Use your time wisely. Those distractions have nothing to do with your dreams. If you are waiting for someone to give you a hand up, it won't happen; if you're waiting for the right moment, it will never come. Do what must be done today so that tomorrow you can work on another aspect of your dream that you want to see fulfilled.

Every achievement, award, degree, or honor will require you to give up something in exchange for what you desire. Sacrifice is more about giving than getting; it is about losing to win, and very few people like to lose. When we are willing to value what we are over what we have, I believe we are achieving success at a higher degree.

On the journey to your success, you will lose part of who you are, just to become who you will be. Losing is a requirement to achieve greatness; it is the core of sacrifice. We must forget our old way of thinking and doing things and understand that new doors require new techniques.

Somewhere in life, there are doors that you have not even dreamed of, and depending on your decisions now, it could lead to the life you have always dreamed of. You will never know how good you are at something until you invest your whole being into it. You must be consumed with the idea and possibilities of your investment.

Remember when you were a kid and how you cherished allowing your imagination to be free? Somewhere during life, you stopped imagining and allowed the difficulties of life to put you in a box. Life happens; however, you must figure out what it is you want out of life before you take off from the runway. Dreaming is important because it stretches the mind and allows you to go where life's limitations have no boundaries.

It is in this place we can forget about the worries of life and rest in the essence of fulfillment without worry or stress. Here we can fly a plane, own a business, bake a cake, or bring world peace. These are not merely wild thoughts; these are the passions of your heart communicating to your mind that there is something inside of you. Starting now, you can wake up from your daily sleepwalk and turn your dreams into reality and live the life you always wanted by finding those dreams you had as a kid and incorporating them into your now.

Muhammad Ali had a famous quote that is still heard around the world today; he said, *"I float like a butterfly and sting like a bee."* The relationship between the two different worlds is far from being believable on the surface until you understand the metaphor and context. Ali's reference was witty and brilliant because he indicated that he moved as light and free as a butterfly, but his punches were quick and hurt like the sting of a bee.

To understand the meaning behind Muhammad Ali's famous words, you first must realize that he was confident in his ability and secondly, he never stopped dreaming. Merriam-Webster's Dictionary defines success *as a degree or measure of succeeding, a favorable or desirable outcome; it could also mean the attainment of wealth, favor, or a position of prominence or superiority.*

This definition overlooks what success is on a small scale and gives a brief understanding on an exceptionally large scale. The important part that is missing in the definition cannot be explained, only experienced. One of the things that we take for granted when we read or see a success story is the details of how success came about.

When you look at a successful person, you don't see the hard times, sleepless nights, setbacks, or the pain of the process. The part of the success that we see is the lights, camera, and action of the achievement. You see beautiful houses, fancy cars, expensive jewelry, and exotic trips. None of these things are a true representation of the mistakes, the ups and downs, or the failures that the person encountered.

Material things are the rewards of hard work. Success is beautiful, but the process is ugly. Success is about learning how to micromanage the little things in life. It's about how to take what you have in your hand and work it till it produces more. The apple tree doesn't produce apples until you plant the seed. Even before you get the apple tree you still must water it and maintain it for it to grow properly.

The seed produces an apple tree because it is in the right soil; it has had the proper maintenance and has been placed in the right environment. Growth takes time; it is a lengthy process that starts underground before you see results on the topsoil.

Having an idea, dream, or goal is like having a seed; it means nothing if you don't understand the process and the time it takes to produce the harvest. The first thing you must find out is what type of seed you have, then you must find out what environment that seed thrives in the best. Your seed is different from the next person's seed; no two seeds are the same.

A few of my good friends are photographers. We all have similar skills but differ in our work. One is just a photographer. One is a DJ and a photographer. One shoots models. One does photography and videography. All of us are from different trees with similar seeds; one person's strain of seed may be more potent than another's.

One of the biggest failures that hinders early success is overlooking key steps and information in the planning phase. The vital areas that are needed to ensure longevity are ignored, which leads to poor decisions based on misguided information. Due to the time that is required, people often ignore sound judgment because it doesn't make dollars or cents.

Money is usually the motive that blinds people because they are thinking about the apples before planting the seed. Knowing what type of seed you have inside of you is crucial because it determines the steps you will need to take to develop a harvest.

Everything you do in life will require some investment. Whether you are working for a paycheck, studying to become a doctor or lawyer, or joining a nonprofit board, it will require time. Success is about investing your time, and it is the one thing we cannot get back. We make time for what we want, not what we need; going to the mall to get your hair, nails, shoes, and clothes are all wants. The honest question to ask yourself is, what do I truly desire?

We adopt ideas and lifestyles from people who have either put in the work or were given an opportunity, and the difference between them and you can be found in their revenue, it exceeds their lifestyle. You are living paycheck-to-paycheck. Yet, you buy $250 sneakers, $95 jeans, and ride in a car with a monthly note that takes half your check. We are struggling to imitate another person's lifestyle who truly can afford to live in it without wondering how they will eat.

Success is about foregoing your temporary pleasures to fulfill your true desires. We have only one life to live, and our time is limited. What do you plan to do with the time you have remaining?

Chapter 14

Finish Strong

The game of life is calling you out right now for a one-on-one matchup, and the stakes are high, its winner take all. You have trained, practiced, and prepared for this moment. Now, it's time to execute your hard work on the court with an outstanding performance. This is not a drill session; this is war. This is for all the times you missed the shot, fumbled the ball; or struck out. This time it's different. It means more than before. It's about being intentional and winning on purpose.

Every experience has been prep work for this moment. You must play like tomorrow is not promised. Leave everything on the field. Remember all the weight you carried during the different seasons of your life when it all seemed like too much to bear, it was merely weight training class. Those very moments were building you up so that you could handle the pressure and difficulties that life would throw your way.

It has all been for your good to build you up mentally, physically, and spiritually to prep you for the journey ahead. Life's hardships are meant to build our faith and strengthen our bond with God. There is nothing too hard for God, and He made a promise that He would never leave you or forsake you.

Just imagine the creator of the heavens and earth telling you that you can handle the weight that you are carrying; that's weight training with purpose. If you can handle the weight you are carrying, then you must understand its intention is not to break you but to build you up.

For every time you have missed the mark, God has given you a second chance. That is the power of grace. Like a great coach, He often puts you on the bench. This helps you learn from your mistakes. It doesn't mean He doesn't love or value you. It means He wants your best. Your best performance in the game of life will always be when there is no time on the clock, and you are under pressure.

There's something about being under pressure that will force you to have a breakout performance. Pressure produces greatness because it causes you to play the game of life with your mind and not with your emotions. When the odds of life are against you, that's when you perform your best; your decisions are sharp and intentional. It seems as if your IQ for the game is enhanced, and your blood is pumping, causing you to feel alive and unstoppable.

When you feel like you're under pressure, you become more confident about your ability, and your vision is clearer on the goals you have set. The more active you become, the better your rhythm becomes; you start to get into the flow of life. What used to seem like a difficult decision to make now becomes second nature, and your passion for achieving becomes more relevant.

No matter where you are in life, you understand the importance of getting to your sweet spot, which are the goals you have put in place to ensure your success. The more we build our relationship with God, who is the head coach, the more we understand what His expectations are for our lives.

Sometimes during the game of life, we fail to hear His voice from all the noise going on. The more we practice spending time with God, the more we ignore the distractions. Situations arise in our lives to teach us how to be more responsive to God's voice and how to drown out the background noise we face through the circumstances of life.

Home field advantage is often like having an extra player on the team; we must learn to take that same mentality with us for the away games of life. You have been chosen by a God who does not lose; every foe He has faced has lost by a huge margin. God's word is our playbook, and if we study the plays, we can have the assurance that victory is the outcome no matter what platform we may find ourselves on.

Spending time with our playbook gives us an advantage in the game of life. When the enemy attacks us in a certain area, we don't have to second-guess our next move. Knowing your playbook equips you to be ready to counter with the right word to defeat the enemy's tricks and schemes. The playbook we have been given is the difference in walking in victory or defeat. Study your playbook and invest the time needed so you can win no matter what you may encounter. We have already been awarded the victory through our Lord and Savior Jesus Christ; however, we still must play the game of life until the final whistle is blown.

Our job is to imitate Christ in all we do, whether we are on the field of sports or in the field of life. Since we have been chosen and called to endure to the end, we should be confident that the promises of God are Yes and Amen. We have been given the power and authority to finish the race and not give up. The great reward that is waiting for us is just beyond the finish line.

There are over 35 scriptures recorded in the bible that reference running. In Habakkuk chapter 2 verses 2 through 3, it says: *"Then the Lord answered me and said, "Write the vision and engrave it plainly on [clay] tablets so that the one who reads it will run. For the vision is yet for the appointed [future] time; it hurries toward the goal [of fulfillment]; it will not fail. Even though it delays, wait [patiently] for it, because it will certainly come; it will not delay."* Though we may fail in certain areas of the race, we have been commanded to continue to run with our eyes on the victory. Though trials may come, and your victory has been delayed, keep fighting, keep believing, and keep running for it will surely come to pass.

One of the greatest college coaches of all time was Dean Smith of the North Carolina Tar Heels. What made Smith a great coach is he built a relationship with every player that he coached. Players were comfortable with Smith on and off the court. That type of relationship helped the coach understand the players, and built trust and confidence.

As a coach, it builds your reputation as a true leader, one who listens and considers the player's thoughts, feelings, and emotions about certain areas of the game. Everyone has a different job and as a team, there is an understanding that the common goal is to win. In the end, the head coach makes the final decision. Everyone, from the staff to the water boy, honors, and respects the leadership. It is a process, and as a Head Coach, Dean Smith understood that to win, he had to become kin to the players on and off the court.

God wants nothing more than to build a relationship with us so that we may learn to trust his leadership for our lives. The more we encounter opposition in our lives, the more we can rely on God's ability to lead us in the good fight.

Only a great coach knows that winning is not just about points; it is about the performance. A one-point win doesn't deserve the same celebration as a 30-point win. The one-point win signifies that there is much work to do, and players do not understand how to fulfill their roles. When a team wins by 30 points, the win shines light on how teamwork brings success. It speaks about the player's confidence in the coach and the coach's confidence in his players.

For example, in basketball, there are two similar shots that produce two different types of reactions. The first shot is a layup; it is as simple as dribbling toward the goal and putting the ball directly in the hoop or using the backboard as a guide to score the basket. On the other hand, there is the dunk, which is a more creative way of putting the ball into the basket. The dunk is about power and authority; it is when a player leaps in the air from a distance and slams the ball into the basket.

Both shot styles score points. One is about fundamentals and ease. The other is about power and authority. They both add points on paper. However, the dunk is about finishing strong. A dunk signifies that a player was intentional about putting the ball in the basket with power and authority; it was done on purpose. God has given us power and authority in our spirit to defeat the enemy and end the game of life strong.

When we look back at the story of Job in an earlier chapter, the enemy didn't attack Job with fundamentals; he attacked Job with power and authority. The enemy was intentional about his work;

he wanted Job to turn his back on God. Sometimes in life, terrible things happen to good people; is it a sign that God doesn't love you? No, it simply means that God believes in your ability to carry the weight of the situation. Even in Job's calamity, he still understood his role and recognized God's role in leadership. He realized that his relationship with God was far more important than all that he had lost.

We often fail to see that in pain there is love. In the process, there is progress. Setbacks are just setups. It is all for our benefit; however, during the process, we often don't see or understand God's ways. Learning to trust God is a process. It's easier said than done. I have faced hardships, setbacks, and heartaches. I never asked for any of it. But God knew what was in me. He knew my gifts and talents were enough to get me through whatever I might face on my journey to the finish line.

There is nothing that you cannot handle; if you are facing it, then you can handle it. Everything that has happened to you has been for the greater good and serves a purpose for the life God has given you. Giving up is not an option. You are not broken, just cracked. The potter can fix your flaws. Once you realize this, you can live in confidence. Your best life lies ahead. Now is the time to decide. Will you stay on the bench of life, watching others celebrate God's goodness? Or will you step up and put on your game face?

Take a few moments and recite this prayer: "*Father, I know you have called me into the game of life. I may not understand where you are guiding me, but I trust your leadership." There is nothing impossible for you, and right now the victory is mine. Give me the strength and courage to do the things that may seem hard. "From this day, I want you to be pleased with my performance. Though I may stumble, I will give you my best, in the mighty name of Jesus Christ. Amen!*"

As you open your eyes, you see the crowd cheering, and you hear music playing, it is your favorite song. The buzzer sounds, and as you look up at the scoreboard, you realize that the score is all tied up, and the final play is designed for you. Someone passes you a water bottle. You take a drink. As the play is being drawn up, you feel a bit more nervous than usual. With time winding down, you realize the importance of this last play.

This is what you have been getting up early for, this very moment, it is why you have sacrificed so much, it is the very reason you spent all your time practicing. Now is the time, the next 30 seconds will change your life no matter the outcome. This is not the time to think about what you will do after the game, next week, or even tomorrow.

Once the whistle blows there will be no going back, no second-guessing, no regrets. Now, all your hard work comes into play. The whistle blows. You walk onto the court. Your opponent shakes his head as if he can stop you. You smile and rub your hands together. As the referee raises his hand and blows the whistle, the defense double-teams you. You take a deep breath and glance at the clock one last time. You realize that no matter what, you must get to the basket and FINISH STRONG!

Chapter 15

Winning With God

As far back as I can remember, my vision for life has been about what I wanted to do and accomplish. Throughout the various stages of life, it has been more about my plans and not the plans that God has set out for His will. About four years ago, I realized that my plans were good but had areas that were full of incomplete endings. Somehow, I had created a list of goals that once completed never ended; they only connected to other goals, leading to no full satisfaction.

All my accomplishments have been God's will for my life, for a greater purpose. Every miracle, blessing, setback, failure, and loss has been about God molding me into who He created me to be—complete and lacking nothing. The people, and situations that broke me on the outside were building me up on the inside. All the heartaches that I experienced were helping me heal; the disappointments happened so that the hurt would produce growth. The setbacks were God's way of protecting me from the dangers ahead that wanted to snuff me out.

Every person who decided to walk away, or whom I walked away from, was God's way of saying, "I AM all you need. Depend on me; I will never let you down, leave you, or forsake you." Looking back, I see God molding me. He has made me sharper and smoothed my rough edges. He has drawn me into a true relationship with His presence. When I was a young kid, my mother would fuss at me about the bonehead mistakes that I would constantly make. At the time, what was in front of me was far more important than where I was headed.

Things had to happen now; being patient was something I wanted no part of. Life was about living in the present; why wait for a future that may not exist? She would always say, "*Son, God has great plans for your life. The only reason the enemy keeps attacking you so hard is that he knows that if you figure out your purpose, you will break the chains that he has been using to hold you back from reaching all that God has for you.*" Somehow, her words would go in one ear and right out the other.

Life was about having fun, and who was God to tell me how to live my life? Not understanding who and what God wanted from me caused me to run away for so long. Thank God for second chances, mercy, favor, and grace, because I was headed down the wrong path like a crash dummy just waiting on impact. Something in my heart and mind changed late in 2013, and I started experiencing God's goodness on my own.

There is something incredible that happens when you have an encounter with God. When my mother passed, so many people she knew shared their own experiences, encounters, and testimonies about how she had impacted their lives. She was always available to listen and lend a helping hand. As a kid growing up, church was more about going because I had to. At the time, I didn't have a choice, my grandmother and mother both attended church faithfully. They were involved in various boards, committees, and choirs for what seemed like my entire life.

My mother served until her time was up; she left a lot of memories and stories behind. For me, church was nothing more than a place where people went to hear singing, shouting, and a man talk for what seemed like forever. At my age as a kid, my mind was far from the world of clapping, singing, and praising God. I had more important things to worry about, like selling drugs, making money, hanging out, and chasing girls. There have always been unexplainable things happening in my life that I never really looked at until later in my adult years.

I remember sitting in a smoke-filled room full of drugs with my best friend who pulled out a gun, points it at random people, and minutes later accidentally shoots himself while sitting right next to me. As a young kid, I have always been mature and found myself hanging around older men who would teach me about the streets.

It was a hot Saturday morning in the middle of summer at my mother's house when the phone rang. My mother knocked on my room door to tell me that a strange man was on the phone and wanted to speak to me. Her first question as she held the phone was what did I get myself into, as she stared at me with a strange look in her eye. At the time, I was high from smoking weed with friends earlier and said, "Nothing," as I laughed.

As I walked down the hallway, I could hear my mother mumbling behind me about how I would learn my lesson one day. When I grabbed the phone off the wall in the kitchen and said, "Hello," a man with a heavy accent warned that "my family would die if he did not get his money." I laughed and hung up the phone. The supplier who had been fronting me drugs to sell was upset. I had been avoiding his calls and jumped the fence on him. That would be my last conversation with him.

Later that evening, I arrived at my friend Low's house. He told me that Kesha, a girl who had a crush on me, had a dispute with the supplier. She shot him in the neck three times. He died instantly. Understand that everything that has happened to me was part of God's process to redirect my focus toward His will.

No matter how much my mother encouraged me to seek God, the farther I found myself running. For me, the idea of God sitting in heaven watching my every move seemed a bit far-fetched. How could the creator of the universe love and care about someone with a heart and a past like mine?

There is a story that paints a beautiful narrative about a father's love. In the book of Luke, chapter 15, verses 11 through 32, there is a story about a father and two sons, and it reads: *"Once there was this man who had two sons. One day the younger son came to his father and said, "Father, eventually I'm going to inherit my share of your estate. Rather than waiting until you die, I want you to give me my share now." And so, the father liquidated assets and divided them. A few days passed, and this younger son gathered all his wealth and set off on a journey to a distant land.*

Once there, he wasted everything he owned on wild living. He was broke; a terrible famine struck that land, and he felt desperately hungry and in need. He got a job with one of the locals, who sent him into the fields to feed the pigs. The young man felt so miserably hungry that he wished he could eat the slop the pigs were eating.

Nobody gave him anything. So, he had this moment of self-reflection: "What am I doing here? Back home, my father's hired servants have plenty of food. Why am I here starving to death? I'll get up and return to my father, and I'll say, 'Father, I have done wrong – wrong against God and against you. I have forfeited any right to be treated like your son, but I'm wondering if you would treat me as one of your hired servants?"

So he got up and returned to his father. The father looked off in the distance and saw the young man returning. He felt compassion for his son and ran out to him, enfolded him in an embrace, and kissed him. The son said, "Father, I have done a terrible wrong in God's sight and in your sight too. I have forfeited any right to be treated as your son." But the father turned to his servants and said, "Quick! Bring the best robe we have and put it on him. Put a ring on his finger and shoes on his feet.

Go get the fattest calf and butcher it. Let's have a feast and celebrate because my son was dead and is alive again. He was lost and has been found." So they had this huge party. Now the man's older son was still out in the fields working. He came home at the end of the day and heard music and dancing. He called one of the servants and asked what was going on.

The servant said, "Your brother has returned, and your father has butchered the fattest calf to celebrate his safe return." The older brother got angry and refused to come inside, so his father came out and pleaded with him to join the celebration. But he argued back, "Listen, all these years I've worked hard for you. I have never disobeyed one of your orders. But how many times have you even given me a little goat to roast for a party with my friends?

Not once! This is not fair! So, this son of yours comes, this wasteful delinquent who has spent your hard-earned wealth on loose women, and what do you do? You butcher the fattest calf from our herd!" The father replied, "My son, you are always with me, and all I have is yours. Isn't it right to join in the celebration and be happy? This is your brother we're talking about. He was dead and is alive again; he was lost and is found again!"

There are some amazing key points in this story; however, we will stick to the one that is the most relevant to our topic. The youngest son's behavior and attitude are often how we act towards God. We have an entitlement syndrome and expect God to do whatever we ask Him to do. Sometimes we beg and plead with God for things that we either don't need or don't deserve.

As a loving Father, God wants the best for us, and He often allows us to have things our way just so we can see that apart from Him, we are nothing. The reason the father in the story gave the sons their fair share of the estate is that it was part of their inheritance and, secondly, because he knew both of his sons.

God truly knows us better than we know ourselves; He knew us long before we were in our mother's womb. He knows our thoughts, behaviors, and actions before we even think to make a move. God knew long before I did that I would run; He knew long before that it would take something life-changing to push me to a breaking point. Isn't it ironic that we get so far gone in our own way that we usually call God when we are down to nothing?

For me, it was here that I realized that apart from God, I can do nothing on my own. Just like the son in the story, no matter how far you go in your actions and behavior, there will come a time when all the fun ends, all your friends leave, and you are all alone. No matter how many times we find ourselves in this place, God wants to greet us with open arms and clean us up. He knows exactly how difficult living this life can be, and even in our stubbornness, He is willing to forgive us.

The things that we desire the most are usually the most harmful to us. What makes this story so vivid and rich with wisdom is because the father never stopped loving and longing to see his son at his best. The power of free will is so incredible, yet it is so dangerous. The consequences of our decisions will either drive us toward our understanding that we need God or drive us away from Him. It is not in God's purpose that one of His children is lost; just like the father in the story, whenever a child of God comes home, God is filled with joy.

There have been plenty of situations throughout my life that I recall thinking just how the son was thinking, "Why am I living this way?" During the son's hardship, he realized who his father was; his father was a great man with many servants. He found himself in a condition that he did not have to be in; he was only there because he felt like his father would not forgive him. Meanwhile, his father kept on living, never forgetting his son; he could only hope that one day his son would come home. The father never left the son; the son decided to leave the father. How familiar does that sound?

God never leaves us; we always leave Him, wise in our own ways, believing that we know more than the one who created us. For me, it was always when things were going good in my life that I didn't need God. Life was good, and I didn't have time to read my Bible, pray, or talk to God.

As soon as the storms of life would come, I would run to my mother or grandmother, looking for help and answers to why all these things were happening to me. Having a relationship with God never really seemed real to me. In tough times, I would search for this being to help me out of my struggles and mess. It never dawned on me that God was always with me, no matter what I did wrong; His presence was like the father in the story, always available, eager, and with open arms. It wasn't until I nearly died that I realized that God was truly real. To be alive after the amount of blood I lost was beyond even the doctors' belief.

It was the words of the doctors that made me realize that God was real. The doctor's exact words were, *"How are you still alive after losing so much blood? It is truly a miracle that you are still alive."* It was my sin that had caused me to be in this position, but God never stopped loving me; He never stopped waiting for me to come back home.

It was the son's ignorance that placed him in the pen with pigs, longing to be satisfied and fulfilled; he chose to go out into the world and find his way, something that we often choose to do, not realizing that in the arms of the father is the best place to be. For me, I had tried to win the game of life without God too many times.

There are plenty of experiences that I could share that truly reflect that a life outside of God is incomplete. Every plan, plot, backdoor, and scheme you can imagine I have tried; there is no other way to live life. Now you could choose to sell your soul for the short-term benefits, but in the end, the value of the deal would be worthless.

One of the beautiful things about the prodigal son's story that is often overlooked is that the passage never mentions the son cleaning up himself before returning home. He went from being in the pen with pigs, daydreaming about food, to realizing who his father was. Once he realized that the pain, hurt, and hunger he was experiencing was really because of his foolish thinking and behavior, it was time to go back home.

The story says he got up and returned home; understand that the condition he was in was not pretty. Can you imagine what he smelled and looked like coming from the pigpen and the trip? That is the beauty of having a loving father; the father was not concerned about how he looked or smelled. The father was more concerned that he came to his senses and made it back home safely. God was never concerned about the environments or conditions I had been in; He has always been more concerned about my safety and return to Him.

The blood of Jesus has healing power and the ability to turn even the filthiest rag clean. There is nothing too hard for God; no matter where you may find yourself, even right now, the love of the Father is always available. When will you realize that life without God is the toughest life you could ever live? God is waiting for you to return so that He can celebrate you.

The life you're currently living is not your best life; all the worrying and sleepless nights are not how God intended you to live. Even right now, as you read these words, if you believe that your life is too far gone for God to ever accept you the way you are, don't be fooled. When you look back at the story of the prodigal son, he not only blew his portion of the inheritance, but his lifestyle was a wild one. In the story, he was far from home; remember, he traveled to a different country. There is nowhere on earth that you can go that is out of the reach of God. The thing that I have come to experience about God is He will meet you where you are.

No matter what you are into, where you've been, or where you are trying to go, God is there, waiting to hear you call. There is nothing to be ashamed of; nobody is perfect; we have all fallen short. The most important thing is that you pick yourself up and turn back to God. You can repent for your sins right where you are, accept Jesus Christ as your Lord and Savior.

The walk is not easy, and though you may stumble, God will never let you fall. Your best life is waiting for you right now; don't hesitate. Decide today to accept the call that God has put on your life. We often become more concerned about how we will look in the eyes of others when the eyes of the Father are all that matters. How much longer will you run from the hand of God? You don't have to experience the worry of tomorrow or the stress of not knowing how you will make it through another setback.

The life that you truly desire is one full of peace, joy, love, gentleness, and steadfastness. Too many times, people assume that life with God is easier, but it's not. Life with God is like working on your game; what you put in it is what you will get out. Winning with God is better than striking out. **YOU WILL WIN!!!**

Made in the USA
Columbia, SC
24 October 2024

44618032R00057